M*A*S*H

TV Milestones

M*A*S*H

David Scott Diffrient

TV MILESTONES SERIES

W

Wayne State University Press   Detroit

12 11 10 09 08   5 4 3 2 1

Cataloging-in-Publication Data

Diffrient, David Scott, 1972–
M*A*S*H / David Scott Diffrient.
p. cm. — (TV milestones)
Includes bibliographical references and index.
ISBN 978-0-8143-3347-1 (pbk. : alk. paper)
1. M*A*S*H (Television program) I. Title. II. Title: MASH.
PN1992.77.M2854D54 2008
791.45'72—dc22

∞ The paper used in this publication meets the minimum requirements
of the American National Standard for Information Sciences—Permanence of Paper
for Printed Library Materials, ANSI Z39.48-1984.

CONTENTS

ACKNOWLEDGMENTS

I would like to thank the staff at the Charles E. Young Research Library at UCLA, especially the accommodating people in the Arts Library Special Collections who assisted me in locating research material in the Larry Gelbart, Burt Metcalfe, and Gene Reynolds files. My sincere thanks also goes to the staff at UCLA's Film and Television Archive who allowed me to watch otherwise unavailable episodes of *AfterMASH*. Dr. Paul Edwards and his staff at the Center for the Study for the Korean War (Independence, Missouri) were helpful in providing resources and documents related to this topic as well. I have drawn inspiration from my former UCLA professor and mentor Vivian Sobchack, whose intellectual rigor and vitality as a media studies scholar continue to astound me. The always-sensible editors at Wayne State University Press, in particular Annie Martin and Barry Keith Grant, were a joy to work with. Finally, the people who mean the most to me—my parents, Donna and Harry Diffrient, and my wife, Hye Seung Chung (who not only watched all 251 episodes of *M*A*S*H* with me but also offered many insights)—have supported my academic work for years, giving me guidance through difficult times. I could not have written this book without their love and steadfast encouragement.

Acknowledgments

*M*A*S*H* in American Popular Culture

Although twenty-five years have elapsed since "Goodbye, Farewell, and Amen" aired on February 28, 1983, time has done little to diminish the significance and influence of CBS's *M*A*S*H* (1972–83), a groundbreaking television series that struggled during its first season (finishing forty-seventh in the ratings for 1972–73) but soon thereafter claimed a mainstream following that ensured success for the next ten seasons. Winning a total of fourteen Emmy Awards (out of ninety-nine nominations), not to mention scores of awards from the Directors Guild of America, the Screen Actors Guild, and the Hollywood Foreign Press Association, *M*A*S*H* has been called "the most popular pre-*Seinfeld* series in television history," a program that, according to several scholars, transformed the medium and brought millions of viewers together as members of an imagined community.[1]

Peggy Herz has called it "the most moral show on TV," one that transcended the generic and stylistic boundaries of the standard sitcom formula to expose, at various times throughout its long broadcast run, racial injustices, gender biases, bureaucratic mishandling, military snafus, and other pressing sociopolitical concerns of the day.[2] Noralee Frankel compares *M*A*S*H* to a bottle of "vintage wine" that has "improved with age," and certainly, off-network syndication has ensured its perennial status, with millions of post–baby boom spectators introduced to the series via reruns aired as part of local stations' daytime and late-night programming.[3] One of the "most potent antiwar statement[s] in American history,"[4] *M*A*S*H* has been translated into fifteen languages and has aired in over twenty-five countries, becoming not only a national institution but also an international phenomenon, as meaningful for people in Australia or Germany as it is for stateside audiences.

However, all this hyperbole should not blind us to the fact that *M*A*S*H* has come under attack for proselytizing and for sanitizing wartime experiences for the sake of commercial entertainment. In contrast to a critic like John Leonard, who believes that "*M*A*S*H* dazzled the sitcom into sentience," Barry Putterman describes this and another CBS series of the 1970s, *All in the Family* (1971–79), as "mid-cult gasbags" that "all but bracket off their little bromides in neon."[5] As an example of that "most blatantly social form" of comedy, satire, *M*A*S*H* was especially lamentable from Putterman's point of view, for it replaced the "outcast horse-play" and intentional infantilism associated with such short-lived, largely forgotten slapstick TV programs as *I'm Dickens . . . He's Fenster* (ABC, 1962–63) and *Valentine's Day* (ABC, 1964–65) with "the smug, moralizing wheezes of doctors and military officers."[6] Whether or not one agrees with Putterman that a "historical inevitability" transformed the televisual landscape for the worse, it is hard to dismiss his argument that a certain self-righteousness pervades the programs made for CBS under Fred Silverman's reign, "quality" TV series like *The Mary Tyler Moore Show* (1970–77), *All in the Family*, and *M*A*S*H*, which collectively marked a shift away from the network's "hick-centric" programming of the 1960s (*The Beverly Hillbillies* [1962–71], *Green Acres* [1965–71], and so forth) toward more "sophisticated" sitcoms that resonated with the urban, upscale audiences of the 1970s.

Perhaps the most strident yet astute criticism directed at *M*A*S*H* comes from the cultural historians Mike Budd and Clay Steinman, who in a 1988 essay attempt to unpack the "institutional and discursive apparatus" of this outwardly subversive yet ultimately conservative series.[7] To neosituationists like Budd and Steinman, both *M*A*S*H* and the middle-class fan culture surrounding the show throughout its original broadcast constituted a "flow," an intermingling of stories and commodities. Such a flow, in their words, "mystified" capital and masked the medium's power to reinforce or reproduce dominant ideological values through a televisual style that was functional, self-effacing, invisible, and thus capable of luring audiences into an apparently three-dimensional space where "realistic" yet outlandish characters "seemed to have a life of their own."[8]

The "capitalization, dematerialization, and idealization" of this "warmedy" (an awkward term used by Budd, Steinman, and other critics to denote a "comedy overlaid with empathetic audience identification") extended even to the lives and celebrity status of the actors who played the show's universally loathed or much-loved characters, from Larry Linville, who was never able to escape his pitch-perfect (if single-note) personification of insufferable neurosis, Major Frank Burns, to Mike Farrell, who parlayed the instant likeability of his B. J. Hunnicutt into a kind of "ethereal glow," lending warmth and sincerity to his offscreen support of the National Coalition to Ban Handguns during the 1980s. The cartoonist Bill DeOre of the *Dallas Morning News* offered his less-than-impressed take on the sentimentality of the series on March 1, 1983 (one day after the finale), when he modified the acronym to read "Mostly Absurd Slanted Hogwash."[9] As is obvious from this quick survey of comments on the show, *M*A*S*H* readily sparks opposing responses: to some

3

viewers, it remains the peak of network television, while to others, it smacks of moral superiority or, perhaps worse, simply "isn't funny." This latter sentiment, certainly debatable, is uttered by a teenaged character in an episode of the retro-nostalgic one-season wonder *Freaks and Geeks* (NBC, 1999), just one of the many recent American television programs that, while indebted to *M*A*S*H* in one way or another, nonetheless make derisive jokes about the show (which are probably lost on their primary viewing audience).

One way of gauging a television program's success and historical significance is to examine its impact on subsequent cultural productions. Several television programs have referenced *M*A*S*H*. This sometimes takes the form of homage, as in several *St. Elsewhere* (NBC, 1982–88) episodes, or parody, as in "Breaking Out Is Hard to Do," an episode of the animated series *Family Guy* (FOX, 1999–) that features an Asian man (whose ethnicity is not specified) firing rockets from his helicopter at the show's protagonists and pretending that he is "shooting at Alan Alda and Jamie Farr" (proclaiming at one point, "Take that, wisecracking meatball surgeons!"). Another way of measuring a TV show's popularity or influence is to look "outside the box" at the amount of ancillary merchandise produced for both hard-core fans and general audiences at the time of its original broadcast. Throughout the run of the series, a number of *M*A*S*H*-related goods—some officially licensed, some illegal knock-offs—could be purchased in specialty shops and department stores and can today be found on the auction block or on eBay. These include flashlights, air fresheners, shot glasses, ceramic TV-shaped salt and pepper shakers, gold-tone bookmarks, Lucite key chains, ViewMaster reels, plastic canteens, action figures, scaled models, and miniature military vehicles. Some of the most popular items during the 1970s and 1980s were *M*A*S*H*-themed jigsaw puzzles, board games, and T-shirts, not to mention a wide range of clothing accessories, from camouflage-print nylon wallets with Velcro attachments, to children's wristwatches, to stainless steel dog tags.

Mothers and fathers shopping for their kids' back-to-school items could pick up camouflage green pencils inside yellow cases with the show's acronymic letters emblazoned on the front. At home, they could sip coffee from their official *M*A*S*H* mugs (diner white and featuring green letters with a red cross) while reading any one of the fourteen novels that make up the "MASH Goes to . . ." series, written—in slapdash fashion—by William E. Butterworth and Richard Hooker (a.k.a. Richard Hornberger, the author of the original 1968 novel). These latter texts were published by Pocket Books beginning in 1973 (with *MASH Goes to Maine*), allowing fans of the television series to read about the further adventures of Hawkeye, Trapper, and the other members of the original 4077 who have managed to make their way to such international locales as London, Montreal, Morocco, Moscow, and Paris (in addition to U.S. cities like Las Vegas, Miami, New Orleans, and San Francisco). Such varied types of memorabilia attest to the depth and breadth of the fan cultures surrounding *M*A*S*H,* a television program whose sponsors (such as Honda, which commissioned posters of the cast members on motorcycles following the final episode) took an active role in promoting both the mobility and likeability of the surgical unit, in addition to participating in the synergistic interplay of converging media forms.

To date, over two dozen English-language books about CBS's landmark medical comedy have been published.[10] However, while there is no short supply of episode summaries, cast interviews, trivia quiz booklets, and even recipe guides,[11] only one of these publications—James W. Wittebols's *Watching M*A*S*H, Watching America: A Social History of the 1972–1983 Television Series*—has attempted to examine this TV classic from a scholarly point of view. A valuable contribution to the field of media studies, Wittebols's text provides ample evidence that *M*A*S*H* accurately reflected the zeitgeist of the 1970s and early 1980s, a time bracketed by two Republican presidencies.[12] For all of its strengths, though, Wittebols's book does not fully address the many contradictions and complexities of the series, which is at once antiauthoritarian and a cultural institution in its own right. Tipping over sacred cows yet often falling back on superficial platitudes and politically correct rhetoric, *M*A*S*H*—over the course of eleven years—flitted almost schizophrenically between comedy and tragedy, satire and sincerity. This oscillation nevertheless effectively distilled Korean War (and Vietnam War) veterans' conflicting experiences while reflecting the often-contradictory attitudes among the mainstream populace about the roles that the U.S. military and CIA were playing at home and abroad throughout the Nixon, Ford, Carter, and Reagan administrations.

Although Wittebols convincingly makes the case that *M*A*S*H* mutated, season-to-season, to accommodate cast changes and reflect the shifting cultural ethos of America as the country left an unpopular war in Vietnam behind only to enter an era of renewed cold war conservatism and political interest in places like Central America and the Middle East, his chronological analysis makes for a somewhat fateful journey through eleven (or, more accurately, ten and a half) seasons of the most dynamic, unpredictable television program of its generation. In this book I have tried to supplement Wittebols's sophisticated study, yet also go beyond it in terms of addressing underlying themes, narrative strategies, and stylistic innovations that have been overlooked by others. A fundamental argument that animates my exploration of key episodes is that *M*A*S*H* and its oft-ridiculed spin-off *After-MASH* (CBS, 1983–84) openly indulged a neoliberalist perspective on the cold war era that acknowledged, rather than masked, the United States' conflicting roles in both building and destroying East and Southeast Asian nations in the name of democracy. In the final analysis, I contend that the series was a cultural phenomenon that resonated with diverse audiences precisely because of its contradictory appeals; its "soft," secular-humanist approach to war and the people of Korea as well as its jujitsu-like jabs at what J. Hoberman has referred to as "empty patriotism, official bombast, and military life."[13]

The most pronounced generic characteristic of *M*A*S*H* in its literary, cinematic, and televisual incarnations is its use of dark comedy to deconstruct sacrosanct or taboo subjects (like death, religion, and sexual promiscuousness) while mocking the military brass as well as the political elite. Indeed, there is a constant stream of wisecracks, puns, and practical jokes in the show that, besides supplying the men and women of Mobile Army Surgical Hospital 4077 with a kind of emotional release valve (one that allows them to "stay sane" in an insane environment), also reveals the underlying absurdity of war. A large portion of this book supplies examples of the ways in which the television series blends humor with humanism, biting satire with populist hope. I explore the ways in which this logic of the ridiculous resonated with the changing ideals of the late 1960s and early 1970s, a period in American history when optimism was giving way to pessimism.

Many critics have already suggested some of the ways in which *M*A*S*H* can be recontextualized and read as an allegorical commentary on the war in Vietnam, which dragged on until 1975 (seasons 3 and 4 of the television series) and generated fierce debates on the home front about U.S. involvement in international affairs. I too pursue such a reading in the opening chapters, although I strive to diversify that approach by weaving in references to other examples of antiwar fiction. But rather than focus wholly on the allegorical implications of the series, I attempt to recuperate its significance as a Korean War text, paying particular attention to its continuous mobilization of Korean characters, iconography, and language (a topic I highlight in the book's final chapter). Between the first and final chapters are sections devoted to such varied themes as trauma, boredom, entertainment, community, sexuality, racism, xenophobia, and benevolence. I have designed this study to take the reader from contextual issues (related to M*A*S*H's creation, reception, and circulation in extradiegetic spheres of marketing and consumption) to textual issues (concerning the series' formal innovations, narrative strategies, and motivic focus on the aforementioned themes).

In short, this book addresses the origins of the TV series, with brief references to Richard Hornberger's 1968 novel and Robert Altman and Ring Lardner Jr.'s 1970 film of the same title; its relationship to another, earlier example of antiwar fiction (Joseph Heller's Catch-22); the unique contributions to antiwar discourse made by the show's "authors" (in particular Alan Alda, Larry Gelbart, Burt Metcalfe, and Gene Reynolds); the largely overlooked experiments in televisual style and narrative structure that its writers and directors made; the reception of the program from its first season to its last; its critically disparaged yet politically progressive spin-off, AfterMASH; and its various extradiegetic permutations in American popular culture (in the form of intertextual allusions in other TV series as well as ancillary merchandise and memorabilia).

Because I approach M*A*S*H from a sympathetic yet critically objective perspective that bridges different cultural backgrounds (American and Korean) and academic disciplines (media studies, cold war history, and East Asian studies), this book not only consolidates vital historical and theoretical approaches to the series but also addresses issues often overlooked by fans and critics. For instance, few scholars have written about M*A*S*H as a Korean War comedy-drama, something that I—as someone deeply invested in Korean cultural history—seek to recuperate and highlight without necessarily diminishing its significance as a commentary on the situation in Vietnam. Moreover, my work makes use of the archival materials contained in the Larry Gelbart, Gene Reynolds, and Burt Metcalfe files at UCLA's Arts Library Special Collections. Indeed, this is the first published study of M*A*S*H to incorporate information derived from the original scripts, memos, personal correspondence, and collected papers of the above writers and producers (some of whom made research trips to South Korea), not to mention the first to delve into the political implications of a television series that did more to inscribe the idea of "Korea" in America's collective unconscious than any other cultural production of the twentieth century.

Chapters 1 through 4 examine the making and partaking of M*A*S*H as a literary, cinematic, and televisual phenomenon, beginning with the 1968 publication of Richard Hornberger's bestselling novel of the same title (minus the asterisks and written under the pen name Richard Hooker). Because limited space prevents me from exploring the cultural phenomenon of M*A*S*H in all of its permutations (including a proposed radio program as well as the vast array of ancillary merchandise that could be purchased in toy stores and gift shops throughout the run of the series), the bulk of my analysis falls squarely on its televisual incarnation, which, as I have mentioned, has thus far sparked only one scholarly study. Besides establishing the conceptual framework with which to buttress my subsequent chapters and case studies, the first third of the book therefore explores the genesis of the TV series, the historical contexts of its original broadcast and eventual syndication, and its reception.

While M*A*S*H was sometimes criticized for being a toned-down, laundered version of the original book and film, its humor—especially during the first four seasons—often relied on the harsh juxtaposition of bloodshed and jokes, usually aimed at warmongering officers like Lieutenant General Robert "Iron Guts" Kelly (James Gregory) and the anticommunist CIA agent Colonel Flagg (Edgar Winter). However, death was never a direct source of humor, and the creators made a conscious decision to refrain from using a prerecorded laugh track during the scenes set in the OR. The ludicrous nature of war and military bureaucracy was, however, a subject of numerous episodes over the course of the show's eleven-year run, including one from the fourth season—"The Late Captain Pierce"—in which a visibly living surgeon learns that he is, according to army records, officially dead. As a kind of Orwellian "un-person," the "deceased" Hawkeye is thus victim to a bureaucratic snafu of the highest order, one that denies him his weekly paycheck and sends shockwaves through his network of friends and family back home in Crabapple Cove. This episode and several like it, with their unremitting focus on mortality and uncertainty, lend *M*A*S*H* a depth of meaning and philosophical insight into thanatological themes that have rarely been explored so compellingly on television.

The sober yet sordid, sensitive yet irreverent tone of the series may not seem as radical today as it did to audiences in America at the time of its 1972 debut, before the war in Vietnam had come to a complete halt and amid governmental scandals and cover-ups such as Watergate. However, because its satiric focus was on the military industrial complex and other dehumanizing institutions that had begun to look ridiculous in the eyes of the disenfranchised and dissatisfied masses, *M*A*S*H* can arguably be called television's "first dark comedy."[14] Although there had been generic predecessors to *M*A*S*H* as early as the mid-1950s, when *The Phil Silvers Show: You'll Never Get Rich* (a.k.a. *Sergeant Bilko*, 1955–59) became a television staple, no other military-focused sitcom—not *McHale's Navy* (ABC, 1962–66), not *McKeever and the Colonel* (NBC, 1962–63), not *Gomer Pyle*,

U.S.M.C. (CBS, 1964–69), and not *Hogan's Heroes* (CBS, 1965–71)—was as satiric as *M*A*S*H,* even if its black humor did gradually give way to feel-good populism during the early Reagan years.

Much has been made of the fact that *M*A*S*H* ran nearly four times longer than the Korean War, which lasted from June 25, 1950, to July 27, 1953.[15] The show's longevity speaks not only to a public consensus built, ironically, on a combination of compassion and dissent, but also to the show's unflagging attention to detail and the long-term dedication of its core group of creative personnel, many of whom worked twelve- and fifteen-hour days of shooting and who, in return, took home armloads of awards for acting, writing, and directing. One celebrated member of that group—Alan Alda—deserves special attention as a contributor both in front of and behind the camera. Fittingly, a large portion of the final section of this book, encompassing chapters 6 through 8, puts special emphasis on Alda's onscreen and offscreen personas, which provide us with the proper epistemological lens through which to view the series' complex treatment of gender, sexuality, and identity, not to mention questions of race and place, the latter made all the more relevant by Hawkeye's paternalistic affection for "local indigenous personnel"—Koreans who may benefit from his benevolence yet rarely have the opportunity to speak for themselves or exert any agency within the MASH unit.

It is important to point out here that the first Mobile Army Surgical Hospitals sprang up after the end of World War II but would not be put to use in a combat situation until the outbreak of the Korean War. Officially organized by the U.S. Army in 1948, MASH units were designed as fully functional hospitals capable of handling large numbers of incoming wounded (transported via helicopter and ambulance) close to the front.[16] Initially consisting of sixty beds each (in addition to Quonset huts and canvas tents for eating, sleeping, and worshipping in) and equipped with the most up-to-date surgical instruments, these medical units represented a modern alternative to the portable evacuation hospitals and battalion aid stations that had been used during the Second World War; while large, they could quickly and efficiently be moved to different locales as part of an evasive tactic ("bugging out"). Although they would undergo design changes over the course of the Korean War and became less mobile as a result of lulls in the fighting, these units retained a strong sense of community for the surrogate families of doctors and nurses therein and remained central to the U.S. military's short-term goal of reducing the number of American causalities as well as its long-term goal of securing stability in the region. Although a MASH unit (the 212th) was sent to Iraq in 2003, the last of these medical organizations stationed in South Korea (the 43rd, formally the 8055th) was decommissioned on June 11, 1997, at a ceremony held at Camp Humphreys, Pyongtaek, and attended by cast and crew members of the television series *M*A*S*H*.[17]

The series, while disparaged by some critics for sugar-coating the experiences of Korean War veterans, has also been credited for bringing the heroic efforts of the real medical personnel to light. Although it certainly deserves recognition for accurately depicting the communal ethos—if not the sexual shenanigans—that existed within the camps,[18] *M*A*S*H* does depart from historical record and the facts surrounding the actual makeup and mobility of these medical units, which each consisted of at least two hundred staff members who were forced to periodically "put it up, take it down, put it up, take it down" throughout the three-year conflict. According to a technical consultant on the series, Otto F. Apel, "mobility was the name of the game. That was a concept we learned well." For Apel and the rest of the men and women in the 8076th, the mantra was "move it, move it, move it."[19]

Another MASH unit, the 8055th, was forced to relocate twenty-seven times during the first sixteen months of the war.[20] Over the course of its eleven-year network broadcast (totaling 251 episodes), *M*A*S*H* depicted this "put it up, take it down" scenario on only three occasions,[21] for reasons that are specific to a long-running TV series whose exterior scenes were filmed at a central location: the Fox Ranch in Calabasas, California (interiors were shot on Sound Stage 9 at Fox). However, what *M*A*S*H* may have lacked in terms of historical accuracy was made up for by the determination of Larry Gelbart, Gene Reynolds, and Burt Metcalfe to creatively parlay documented wartime experiences into a heightened form of "mediated realism" contingent on the behind-the-scenes involvement of actual surgeons as well as the onscreen antics of a largely *stationary*, rather than mobile, unit (modeled after the MASH 8055th) to which we, the audience, return each week.[22] The creators and producers of the show not only checked for accuracy by using a 1950 Sears Roebuck catalog but also drew historical details from William L. White's book *Back Down the Ridge*, an account of "the process a wounded man goes through" in being transported "from an aid station to a M*A*S*H unit, then to Japan."[23] Moreover, they sought out and consulted medical advisers, such as Dr. Walter Dishell, who monitored dialogue and ensured that the scripts adhered as closely as possible to the particular patois—the unique forms of speech or wartime vernacular—put to both practical and poetic use by veterans of the Korean conflict.[24] It is to those individuals, the men and women who risked their lives stitching up wounded soldiers and civilians in the Korean War, that this book is dedicated.

A Novel Idea and an Unconventional War Film

To tell the story of *M*A*S*H* as a televisual phenomenon, it is necessary to first reflect on its literary and cinematic forerunners, which anticipated many of the themes that would be cultivated and treated with greater sensitivity and complexity during the program's eleven-season run on CBS. So, let us now turn our attention to that best-selling antiwar novel from 1968, which set the satiric tone adopted in Robert Altman's film of the same title two years later and in the award-winning television series that Larry Gelbart, Gene Reynolds, and Burt Metcalfe subsequently produced throughout the 1970s and early 1980s.

Written by Dr. Richard Hornberger under the pen name of Richard Hooker as a semi-autobiographical portrait of his time in South Korea, *MASH: A Novel about Three Army Doctors* (note the lack of asterisks) combined the author's personal reminiscences of actual events and real people with fictionalized dramatizations and characterizations.[1] Initially rejected by more than a dozen publishing houses, Hornberger's manuscript made its way into the offices of William Morrow, the New York–based company that in October 1968 published this raucous story of free-spirited surgeons who take to booze and hit the links to escape the daily horrors surrounding them. Part of a cultural trend in English-language publishing, *MASH* rode a wave of success based on word-of-mouth recommendations and contributed to the rise to a new generic dominant during the 1960s: the antiwar novel, earlier epitomized by Joseph Heller's *Catch-22* (1961).[2]

Like the film and television adaptations that followed, Hornberger's novel focuses on the men and women who work twelve-hour shifts at a fictional Mobile Army Surgical Hospital, the 4077, located dangerously close to the front lines and about twenty-five miles away from the next MASH unit (the 6073). Of these individuals, three in particular—Benjamin Franklin "Hawkeye" Pierce, "Trapper" John McIntyre, and Augustus Bedford "Duke" Forrest—stand out as the main protagonists. These skirt-chasing doctors quickly develop an antagonistic relationship to the "regular army" types represented by Major Johnathon Hobson, Captain Frank Burns, and Major Margaret Houlihan. That hostility distinguishes the trio as countercultural heroes willing to risk being court-martialed for the sake of a good practical joke. It is Hawkeye, though, who occupies the most prominent spot in the loosely episodic plot, effectively suturing the strands of the narrative together through his bemused observations about the chaos and calamity engulfing the camp (which is nevertheless kept running smoothly by the diminutive Corporal "Radar" O'Reilly). This privileging of Hawkeye would eventually shape the textual contours of the television program, which—although an ensemble series filled with nearly a dozen talented character actors—is really Alan Alda's show (both in front of and behind the cameras). In fact, many biographical details concerning Hawkeye, who would undergo significant changes over the course of the TV series' eleven seasons, are provided in the first chapter of Hornberger's book. It informs us, for instance, that Pierce hails from Crabapple Cove, Maine (the actual birthplace of the author), and that his unusual nickname derives from James Fenimore Cooper's 1826 novel *The Last of the Mohicans* (his father's favorite book).

Readers are introduced not only to Hawkeye but also to Duke in the novel's opening chapter, which provides the first of many peeks behind the door of tent number six ("The Swamp") and offers details about these doctors' family histories and cultural backgrounds. Although coming from two different regions of the United States (Maine and Georgia), Hawkeye and Duke form an immediate bond because of their similar ages (both are in their late twenties) and their shared insolence in the face of military bureaucracy and hypocrisy. This attitude casts in relief the sanctimonious demeanor of Hobson, another character brought to light in chapter 1. Prone to prayer and subjected to practical jokes, this rather inept thirty-five-year-old chest surgeon represents an easy target for his younger tent mates. In chapter 2 of the novel, he is honorably discharged from service by Lieutenant Colonel Henry Blake following a skirmish with Duke (who earlier tackled the nincompoop). In Hobson's absence, several other characters make their way to the 4077. Scrawny and enigmatic (as opposed to Wayne Rogers's sturdy and straightforward portrayal in the TV series), Trapper John arrives from Boston in chapter 3, partially concealed behind layers of parka and hesitant to say much about himself, letting his skills in the OR do most of his talking. Quickly gaining a reputation in the MASH unit as a top-notch "cutter," he finally drops his guard once Hawkeye remembers that McIntyre had been an old football rival during their college years.

Chapter 4 ushers Father Patrick Mulcahy into the spotlight. Also known as "Dago Red" (because of the color of his hair), this man of the cloth is a less charitable and kindhearted soul than the camp chaplain who would become such a beloved figure in the television series. As in the film version, it is Dago Red who informs us that Hawkeye and his cohorts—unlike the enlisted men and women—were *drafted* into the Army Medical Corps. Joining Mulcahy on the religious front is a character unique to Hornberger's novel, "Shaking" Sammy, a Protestant preacher whom Hawkeye and Trapper so dislike that they decide to "sacrifice" him; that is, they threaten to make a human Molotov cocktail out of the "holy roller" by tying him to a wooden cross in a mock ritual designed to scare the God *out* of him.

Another subversive act of sacrifice surfaces in chapter 5, which is devoted to the "Painless Pole" Walter Koskiusko Waldowski and his unsuccessful attempt to commit suicide. As the camp's dentist, Captain Waldowski has a special relationship to the other medical personnel in the camp, mitigating the oral pain he inflicts on them by running a round-the-clock poker table out of his tent. Blessed with a reputation for being physically well endowed, he becomes depressed and fears that he might be homosexual after a string of unsuccessful sexual encounters with several nurses. "I think that it's dead," Walt at one point states, referring to his penis (known throughout the camp as the "Pride of Hamtramck"). This grief between the sheets is what leads him to consider taking his own life in an elaborate, Last Supper-like ritual involving a black capsule that, when ingested, merely knocks him unconscious (leaving Painless worry-free and refreshed the next morning).

The book's main cast of characters is completed with the addition of Captain Frank Burns and Major Houlihan in chapter 6. A member of the Army Nurse Corps, the forty-year-old "femme fatale" Houlihan earns the nickname "Hotlips" after her late-night rendezvous with Burns is broadcast over the camp's loudspeaker (thanks to a strategically placed microphone under their bed). Like Hobson before them, Houlihan and Burns are made the butt of practical jokes. However, while the Chief Nurse is eventually accepted by the Swampmen, Burns is sent packing for the States after he hurls a coffee pot at Hawkeye. Besides them, other minor characters appear for the first time in these middle sections of the book, such as the "bedpan jockey" Private Boone, the anesthesiologist Captain "Ugly" John Black, the respected surgeon Roger "the Dodger" Danforth, and the seventeen-year-old Korean houseboy Ho-jon, who has been drafted by the army and whom Hawkeye is eventually able to send to his alma mater back in the States (Androscoggin College) after raising money for the tuition.

This paves the way for another altruistic endeavor on Hawkeye's and Trapper's part, depicted in chapter 8. Asked by a U.S. congressman to fly to Japan and operate on his injured son, the so-called pros from Dover arrive there—golf clubs in tow—only to focus their attention on a patient in greater need of their services, a Japanese-American orphan who is tended to and subsequently adopted by Hawkeye's old friend "Me Lay" Marston (an American anesthesiologist stationed in Kokura).

Such displays of American benevolence are in keeping with Hawkeye's humanitarian values and are only partially offset by his having earlier generated the necessary revenue for Ho-jon's education through a "sacrilegious" staging of the Passion Play. With Trapper John cast as a crucified Jesus Christ, Hawkeye sold autographed photos of "the Lord" to American GIs at a dollar apiece. This plus the references in chapter 11 to an "epileptic whore" at Mrs. Lee's house of prostitution (who has convulsions each time she services a client) are the most controversial elements in Hornberger's novel, which is otherwise devoted to medical procedures and male-dominated sports such as football and golf—two pastimes pursued by the doctors toward the end of the novel.

Once Hawkeye and Trapper return to the 4077 after their trip to Japan, they encounter a sharp increase in the number of casualties, operating on everyone from a Turkish soldier to a Puerto Rican kid to a Dutch private to a Chinese prisoner of war. Given the endless supply of incoming wounded ("black, white, yellow—friend and foe," whose "bellies, chests, necks, arteries, arms, legs, eyes, testicles, kidneys, [and] spinal cords, all shot to hell,"[3] are beginning to blend into one corporeal nightmare for the surgeons), it is not surprising that Hawkeye, Trapper, and Duke should welcome new additions to the camp; first a surgeon named Captain Bridget McCarthy from Boston (a female forerunner of Major Charles Emerson Winchester III in the television series), then Colonel DeLong (Blake's temporary replacement), and finally Captain Oliver Wendell "Spearchucker" Jones (an African American neurosurgeon who had once been a professional football player). Of these latter three characters, only Jones—who is brought in from the 72nd Evacuation Hospital in Taegu and used as a secret weapon in the 4077's victorious scrimmage against General Hammond's football team—would appear in the cinematic adaptation.

The novel's twelfth chapter delves into the prejudice and racism that Jones has encountered as an African American doctor stationed in Korea. Jones's self-described "black man's burden" is exacerbated by those "goddamn phonies . . . who knock themselves out to show you that your color doesn't make any difference, and if it wasn't for your color they wouldn't pay any attention to you."[4] The initial tension between Jones and Duke, a Southerner who refers to the new arrival as a "nigra," is one of the most interesting passages in the book, a potentially explosive encounter that is significantly diffused in the cinematic adaptation because Forrest is sidelined throughout the latter half of the film, which nevertheless culminates—like the novel before it—with him and Hawkeye receiving news that they are shipping out soon (leaving Trapper John behind, since he has "six months of servitude still ahead of him").

"Not since *Catch-22* has the struggle to maintain sanity in the rampant insanity of war been told in such outrageously funny terms." So went the book jacket blurb penned by Ring Lardner Jr., the once blacklisted screenwriter who first read Hornberger's novel when it was in galley form a few months before it was published in 1968. Decades earlier, Lardner had written screenplays for such celebrated studio-era classics as *Woman of the Year* (1942), *Laura* (1944), and *Forever Amber* (1947) before being singled out by the House on Un-American Activities Committee (HUAC) in the late 1940s as one of the Hollywood Ten. His career a casualty of the McCarthy-era witch hunts, he was sentenced to a year in prison for his communist affiliations and blacklisted by studio heads. At the age of fifty-three, Lardner saw *M*A*S*H* as a means of reclaiming his place in the industry while remaining true to his political beliefs, and he was so smitten with Hornberger's unconventional war story that he immediately drafted a screenplay and sent it to Ingo Preminger, his former agent.

The brother of Otto Preminger, Ingo saw great potential in Lardner's treatment and forwarded it to David Brown and Richard Zanuck, who were then in charge of Twentieth Century-Fox (ironically, the studio that had fired the blacklisted writer in 1947). They likewise understood the value of the material and, after buying the movie rights to Hornberger's book for $100,000, approached over a dozen different directors (including George Roy Hill, Stanley Kubrick, Sidney Lumet, Mike Nichols, Arthur Penn, Sydney Pollack, and Franklin Schaffner, all of whom were either too busy to do the film or indifferent to the idea) before finally agreeing to hire Robert Altman—a longtime director of television episodes—for the job.

The forty-four-year-old Altman, a former air force lieutenant who had nurtured the idea of making a farcical film about World War I flyers called *The Chicken and the Hawk* (which never got off the ground), was initially hesitant about the project given the "racist" aspects of the original book and the "dreadful" quality of Lardner's script.[5] But the maverick auteur, who had already earned recognition in Hollywood as the director of *Countdown* (1968), from which he was fired by Jack Warner of Warner Bros., and *That Cold Day in the Park* (1969), relented once he realized that *M*A*S*H* might offer him an opportunity to bring his much-delayed war film project to fruition while slyly commenting on the situation in Vietnam.[6] With this in mind, he began piecing together a large stock company of actors including recognized talents like Robert Duvall, Elliott Gould, and Donald Sutherland (who were suggested by Ingo Preminger) as well as newcomers from television and theatre such as David Arkin, René Auberjonois, Roger Bowen, Tim Brown, Bud Cort, Michael Murphy, and Tom Skerritt. These and other performers would lend the already sprawling story even greater dimension through structured improvisations before the camera. Beginning in April 1969, Altman and his stock company camped out at Fox's Lake Malibu ranch in the Santa Monica Mountains, where filming commenced without studio interference.

Although Altman frequently fills the widescreen frame with peripheral characters, two in particular—Donald Sutherland's "Hawkeye" Pierce and Elliott Gould's "Trapper" John McIntyre—take center stage throughout this story of martini-sipping draftee surgeons trying to make the best of a bad situation. Besides them, all the other major characters in the novel—Duke Forrest (Tom Skerritt), Frank Burns (Robert Duvall), Margaret Houlihan (Sally Kellerman), Henry Blake (Roger Bowen), Father Mulcahy (René Auberjonois), Radar O'Reilly (Gary Burghoff), "Spearchucker" Jones (Fred Williamson), the "Painless" Pole (John Schuck), and Lorenzo Boone (Bud Cort)—appear in the film.[7] And while its shaggy narrative is once again set during the Korean War, Altman and Lardner intended the film to be a blatant criticism of the fighting in Vietnam, which—by the time of *M*A*S*H*'s January 25, 1970, theatrical debut—had divided

Americans along ideological faultlines and political affilia-tions.[8] Regardless, in both the novel and the motion picture there are several references to Korea, including early attempts by the doctors to send Ho-jon (the Korean houseboy who serves cocktails in The Swamp) to the States. However, as I will show in the ensuing chapters, the underlying "Korean-ness" of M*A*S*H did not truly emerge until the television series was put into production by Twentieth Century-Fox.

Before the film's 1970 release, the studio had weathered one box-office flop after another and was thought to be out of touch with the youth market. In the span of just three years, the company's aging chairman and CEO, Darryl F. Zanuck, had witnessed the big-budget comedy-musicals Dr. Doolittle (1967), Star! (1968), and Hello, Dolly! (1969) sink under the weight of their ambitions and fail to turn a profit. Zanuck's son, Richard, who was then president of the com-pany, was forced to resign by the Fox board of directors in De-cember of 1970, the year the studio lost nearly $80 million and was, according to Douglas Gomery, "on the verge of hav-ing to declare bankruptcy." In The Hollywood Studio System, Gomery discusses this stockholder shakeup in detail and ex-plains that the Annapolis graduate and Rhodes Scholar Den-nis Stanfill replaced Zanuck as chairman of the board.[9] Stan-fill, along with the newly appointed president Gordon Stulberg, inherited the two films that helped wash away some of the struggling studio's red ink: M*A*S*H and Patton (1970). These very different motion pictures were joined by another, less profitable (but more expensive) war film pro-duced by Twentieth Century-Fox that year, Tora! Tora! Tora! (1970).

As an ideological corrective or counterbalance situated opposite these latter two Fox war epics (especially Patton, which relished in the kind of hagiographic hero-worship that was reminiscent of Hollywood's classic World War II films), Altman's M*A*S*H was a commercial and critical breakthrough, third only to Universal's *Airport* and Paramount's *Love Story* that year at the domestic box office. It won the prestigious Palme d'Or at the Cannes Film Festival and the Best Picture Award from the New York Films Critics Circle. It also garnered five Academy Award nominations, including an Oscar win for Lardner Jr. (Best Writing, Screenplay Based on Material from Another Medium). The fact that this unconventional film, which had been made for roughly half of its $3.5 million budget and had even flirted with an "X" rating before its triumphant first screening in a three-thousand-seat San Francisco theater, ended up being one of the highest grossing motion pictures of 1970 (raking in roughly $73 million), is evidence of the general distrust among the populace for government officials and military leaders at that time. It is also a testament to motion picture audiences' increased interest in nontraditional forms of narrative, especially when wedded to a countercultural sensibility.

Besides his trademark use of improvisational performances, overlapping dialogue, ambient sound, widescreen cinematography, fog filters, and the zoom lens, Altman's revisionist approach to the war-film genre is worth noting, not only because it anticipates his subsequent deconstructions of the western (*McCabe and Mrs. Miller,* 1971), the hardboiled detective film (*The Long Goodbye,* 1973), and the backstage musical (*Nashville,* 1975), but also because the film's generic hybridity, tonal schizophrenia, and crisscrossing plotlines seem to have later influenced the creators of the television series. As the next chapter illustrates, Gelbart, Metcalfe, and Reynolds partially retained the film's unblinking depiction of hospital gore, its privileging of rebellious personalities, its celebration of libation and other forms of hedonistic activity, its playful display of sexual foreplay, its iconoclastic take on military authority and religious hypocrisy, and its antiestablishment attitude, which appealed to audiences within the counterculture during and immediately after the Vietnam

War era. If the series did not exploit the Rabelaisian connotations of such things as forcefully as did Altman's film, its emphasis on traumatized bodies and the graphic display of the doctors' blood-smeared smocks made it all the more extraordinary as an example of television "dramedy."

Chapter 2
Big Ambitions for the Small Screen

William Self, Richard Berger, and other studio executives
at Twentieth Century-Fox wanting to cash in further
on the critical and commercial success of Altman's *M*A*S*H*
sent Gene Reynolds the original novel and asked the former
child actor-turned-television producer to create a pilot
episode based on the antics of the 4077 medical personnel.
Having not only served in the United States Navy during
World War II but also worked as an actor during the studio
system era and honed his skills behind the camera on an earlier Twentieth Century-Fox television project, *Room 222*
(ABC, 1969–74), Reynolds intuitively understood the
strengths and weaknesses of the source material. He knew
that if a TV version of both the book and the filmed adaptation were to succeed on the small screen, it would be necessary to bring a talented screenwriter on board, someone who
likewise appreciated the medium's unique capacity to at once
comfort and challenge millions of viewers on a weekly basis.

In 1971 Reynolds contacted Larry Gelbart, an old friend
who had been living in England for nearly ten years. Decades
earlier, Gelbart had worked for the Armed Forces Radio Network and then, after World War II, cut his teeth as a joke

writer for Fred Allen, Sid Caesar, Jack Carson, Bob Hope, and Danny Thomas, among other legendary comedians of stage and screen. Hope had encouraged Gelbart to transition to television work during the 1950s, although Gelbart's most famous pre-M*A*S*H gig was as a cowriter (with Burt Shevelove) of the Broadway musical *A Funny Thing Happened on the Way to the Forum,* which debuted in 1962. It was almost exactly ten years after the spectacular success of *Forum* that Gelbart was called on by Reynolds to return to the United States and collaborate on a television series that would eventually become both men's greatest claim to fame.

After agreeing to coproduce the pilot, which the CBS head of programming Fred Silverman had expressed early interest in, Gelbart went to work on the teleplay in mid-June of 1971, emphasizing certain characters in the novel while eliminating others (such as Duke Forrest). The story that he and Reynolds finally settled on was based on a plotline that had been largely omitted from Altman's film, one that revolved around Hawkeye's efforts to raise money to send Ho-jon to college in the United States. The duo pitched this idea to Alan Wagner, head of development at CBS, who gave them the green light to move forward on production.

Having brought the casting director Burt Metcalfe onboard as associate producer, Gelbart and Reynolds realized that their most difficult challenge lay not in balancing creative responsibilities and individual contributions but rather in retaining the satirical spirit of both the novel and film while toning down the latter's most explicit content: the profanity and artery-spurting surgical scenes as well as the sexual promiscuousness and fleeting glimpses of female nudity. They knew that certain iconographic staples of the motion picture, such as the public address speaker (which had linked the otherwise disconnected vignettes), would carry over into the television version. They decided that certain minor characters in the earlier versions, such as Frank Burns, would need to be fleshed out more fully, and it was quickly agreed that one actor from the original film—Gary Burghoff, who played the clairvoyant and resourceful company clerk Corporal Walter "Radar" O'Reilly (so named because of his extrasensory perception)—would be hired to reprise his role for the small screen.

Their first choice for the role of Captain "Hawkeye" Pierce was Alan Alda, an up-and-coming actor who had begun earning critical recognition for his work on stage and screen.[1] Before M*A*S*H, Alda had performed in a number of plays on and off Broadway. Even before attending Fordham University (where he majored in English), Alan had followed his father into show business, the two of them performing Abbott and Costello routines at the Hollywood Canteen.[2] At the age of sixteen, Alda segued into a semiprofessional career, appearing in summer stock with a small community theater in Barnesville, Pennsylvania. But it was only after graduating with his bachelor's degree in 1956 and marrying Arlene Weiss the following year that Alda really began dedicating himself to acting. He developed the improvisational skills that would serve him so well in M*A*S*H while training at Paul Sill's Second City group in New York.[3] In 1960 he landed his first lead role in the Broadway production of *Purlie Victorious*, and three years later he made his big-screen debut in the filmed adaptation of that play, *Gone Are the Days*.

He began guest-starring in a few episodes of such television series as *The Phil Silvers Show* (CBS, 1955–59), *Route 66* (CBS, 1960–64), and *The Nurses* (CBS, 1962–65) and would achieve greater notoriety in 1964 as one of the recurring cast members in the American version of *That Was the Week That Was* (NBC, 1964–65), alongside David Frost, Henry Morgan, and Buck Henry. In 1968, the same year Hornberger's *MASH* was published, Alda appeared in the motion picture adaptation of George Plimpton's *Paper Lion,* a nonfictional account of the unathletic author's pathetic experience of trying out for

Alan Alda as Captain Benjamin "Hawkeye" Pierce

the Detroit Lions football team. Directed by Alex March, this film is significant insofar as it provides a glimpse not only into the players' locker-room, where normative codes of masculinity and physical prowess cast in relief Alda's scrawniness and lankiness (at 6'2"), but also into the mindset of athletes whose sole purpose on the football field is to *win*—a conceit that both Hornberger and Robert Altman linked to America's military endeavors overseas, whether in Korea or in Vietnam, toward the end of their respective works.

When Alan Alda received Gelbart's script for the pilot episode of *M*A*S*H*, the actor was busy working on another filmed adaptation: a made-for-TV movie titled *The Glass House*. Based on Truman Capote's novel of the same title, this 1972 docudrama was shot at the Utah State Prison, where Alda's character—a professor of political science named Jonathan Paige—has been sent after a conviction of manslaughter (which, through traumatic flashbacks, is revealed to be an accident). Although Paige is introduced to us as a "college professor" (words uttered by a corrections officer on the bus taking him to prison), he is later referred to as a "fag" by Hugo Slocum (Vic Morrow), the worst member of a gang of inmates who go out of their way to express their "manliness" in stereotypical ways, through denigrating anyone who does not fit the traditional mold of masculinity.

As a brutal depiction of the violence, hardships, and corruption that run rampant in many state correctional systems, *The Glass House* may seem remote from the diegetic world of *M*A*S*H*. But this film anticipates some of the central images and main themes within the television series, from the shot of Paige working at the prison pharmacy (dressed in white lab jacket and handing out medication) to the idea that someone who has been dropped into an unfamiliar and dangerous place must rely upon his instincts and intelligence if he is to survive. Like the Korea that is depicted in *M*A*S*H*, the prison is a place where "sometimes it's harder getting mail

31

than not getting mail," a statement Paige makes at one point to another ill-fated inmate, but that could just as likely have been uttered by the other equally clever and disconsolate character Alda played that same year: Hawkeye.

After getting reassurance from Gelbart and Reynolds that their intentions were serious and that the television series would not treat the subject of war merely as an excuse for comedy, Alda signed on and began shooting twenty-four hours after production on *The Glass House* had wrapped. Alda inherited the role of Hawkeye from his cinematic predecessor, Donald Sutherland, and transformed the "everyman" character into a truly exceptional individual—a dedicated surgeon who likes to imitate Groucho Marx and spontaneously bursts into Broadway songs, someone who can cut through the tension of the OR with a perfectly timed zinger (often at Burns's expense) but can just as swiftly segue into a poignant speech about the absurdity of war. With a wit as sharp as his scalpel and a preternatural ability to sniff out military snafus, he can be seen as the wisecracking, thought-provoking screen surrogate for Larry Gelbart, a writer known for colorful colloquialisms and creative turns of phrase that often underline paradoxes in contemporary American society. Referred to as a "crazy agnostic" by Father Mulcahy (William Christopher), Hawkeye may be skeptical of religious dogma, but he remains patient with his patients who frequently turn to God for guidance and amphetamines for pain relief.[4] It is only in the company of military blowhards, whom he staunchly refuses to salute, that Alda's character goes ballistic, antagonistically egging on his opponents in his own inimitable version of "war"—a war of words, ideas, and values instead of rockets or bullets.

Hawkeye's partner in crime, Trapper John McIntyre, is played by Wayne Rogers in the TV series. Like his tent mate, Trapper is a hard-drinking womanizer, yet he too is passionate about his job. Although Rogers eventually left the show at the end of the third season (after which his skirt-chasing character was replaced by Mike Farrell's more wholesome doctor, Captain B. J. Hunnicutt), there is in nearly every episode of M*A*S*H a strong sense of camaraderie between two men whose complex, somewhat asymmetrical relationship recalls the hero-sidekick binary in another early 1970s "buddy show," *The Odd Couple* (ABC, 1970–75). Indeed, there are traces of Felix Unger (Tony Randall) and Oscar Madison (Jack Klugman) in Hawkeye and Trapper, and Alda's character suggests a culturally sophisticated and "brainy" counterpart to Rogers's workmanlike role as the somewhat slovenly "brawn" in the Swamp.[5] The "workplace marriage" of Hawkeye and Trapper—the former linked to intellectual acuity and the latter indicative of physical strength—is thus an offshoot of that domestic sitcom produced two years earlier by Garry Marshall (who adapted Neil Simon's stage play).[6]

Whereas Hornberger's Hawkeye—like Duke Forrest, a "third wheel" who was conveniently left out of the television series—has two children and is married, the TV version of this central character is not saddled with such familial responsibilities and is thus free to engage in flirtatious relationships with nurses while forging a strong fraternal bond with Trapper (and later B.J.) that at times approaches marital status. That partnership, however, is tilted toward one side, in accordance with Alda's increasingly active role behind the scenes as creative consultant (he eventually wrote and directed several episodes, beginning with "The Longjohn Flap" in season 1). One reason Rogers opted to leave the production after its third season was because of a contract dispute. Another reason was that so much media attention was focused on Alda, who was getting better lines and being given more to do in each successive script throughout the second and third seasons. But Alda's centrality to M*A*S*H—while much more apparent toward the end of the series—could be detected from day one, as evidenced by the pilot episode's privileging of Hawkeye as an enunciative agent whose thoughts, words, perceptions, and sensibilities inform the narrative (and our interpretation of it) as no other character's do.

Hawkeye's spoken narration ties together various elements in the pilot episode, the final draft of which Gelbart completed in September of 1971. As Jay Malarcher states, this pilot, "perhaps more than any other single episode, reflects Gelbart's approach to the material . . . its components provid[ing] an understanding of Gelbart's past and future techniques and strategies."[7] One of the most frequently used narrative strategies throughout the eleven-season run of M*A*S*H would be the "Dear Dad" conceit that informs this and several other episodes.[8] This device hinges on an act of letter-writing, which provides the doctor an opportunity to get things off his chest, to gather his thoughts, and compose a piece of correspondence that foregrounds Hawkeye's (and, by extension, Gelbart's) unique phraseology while also reminding us that the home front—while invisibly offscreen—is as much a part of this series as is the battlefront.[9] The fact that this epistolary staple of the series was in place from the very beginning not only indicates just how consistent and cohesive M*A*S*H was throughout the 1970s (despite the major cast changes and character modifications) but also underlines the primacy of the storytelling act, as rendered by Hawkeye, the governing sensibility of the series.

Like its cinematic predecessor, the TV series, which began filming during the last weeks of 1971, was shot partially at the Fox Ranch (while interiors were filmed on Stage 9 of the Fox studios in Beverly Hills)—about as far away as one could get from Korea. Unlike the film, however, the show deals with the war in an intimate and humane way, albeit often by belittling or infantilizing the Korean populace. This is especially true of the pilot episode, which portrays Ho-jon as a poor houseboy in need of American protection and guidance. Ultimately, the television series would evince a more complex understanding of the Korean War and a more respectful treatment of the local people than does Altman's film. It would focus neither on the military elite nor on the GIs in the trenches, although these figures often appeared. Instead, the men and women of Mobile Army Surgical Hospital 4077 take precedence, their day-to-day trials, tribulations, and tricks on one another presented like a never-ending string of plays in the Theatre of the Absurd. In addition to these dedicated surgeons and nurses are the many wounded soldiers and villagers who arrive by ambulance, jeep, bus, or—in the show's most famous image—helicopter, only to be patched up and sent back into the action (or put in harm's way, in the case of the locals).

That iconographic medivac helicopter appears at the beginning of every *M*A*S*H* episode, save for this pilot, the first shot of which is an extreme close-up of a golf tee planted in the ground. A hand descends from the top of the frame and places a golf ball on the tee. An iron then enters from the left side of the frame before the camera pulls back to reveal—in medium-long shot—Trapper John swinging the club while Hawkeye and Ho-jon watch nearby. At this point, an odd caption overlays the image: "Korea, 1950, a hundred years ago." These exterior shots are suddenly juxtaposed with an interior scene. In medium close-up, Henry Blake (McLean Stevenson) and a nurse in medical cap and gown appear to be operating on someone or something just below the frame. The next shot shows a dozing Father Mulcahy (played here for the first and only time by George Morgan), who mechanically crosses himself in sleep as an army truck passes before him.

From there, the scene cuts to a shot/reverse-shot of Margaret Houlihan (Loretta Swit) and Frank Burns (Larry Linville) sitting opposite one another at a table, each silently reading passages of the Bible with intense interest. The camera zooms in to expose, just under the table, Margaret's bare

35

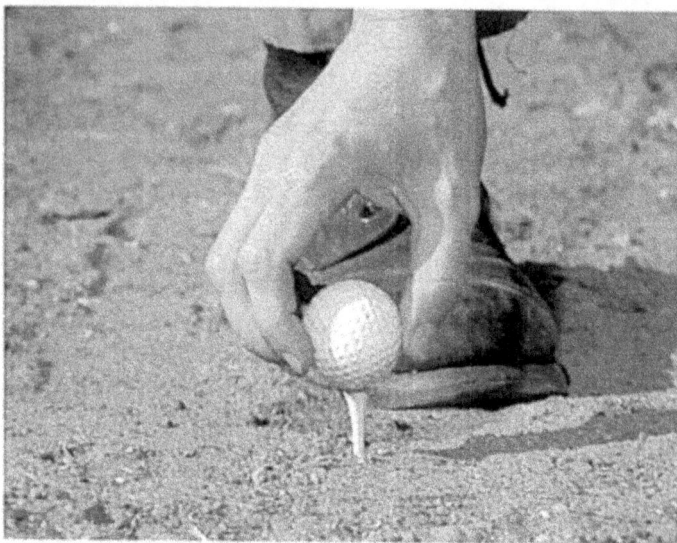

Putting us in place: the first image in the pilot episode

feet caressing those of Frank, the first of many flirtatious moments in the series that discredit their apparent religious fervor. The next shot shows "Spearchucker" Jones (Timothy Brown) playing football with Radar O'Reilly and another enlisted man. A shot of Henry and the nurse in midoperation reveals their "patient" to be a champagne bottle, not a person, and they burst into smiles when it finally uncorks. We then see Trapper John hitting another golf ball, which lands in an adjacent minefield and triggers an explosion. Dramatically, the shot cuts to an image of Radar catching the football and turning on his feet 180 degrees, toward the camera. Sensing something in the air, he declares, "Here they come!" Then, from over Radar's shoulder, we see two MASH choppers emerging above the mountains, accompanied by the melodic strains of Johnny Mandel's lilting theme music, "Suicide is

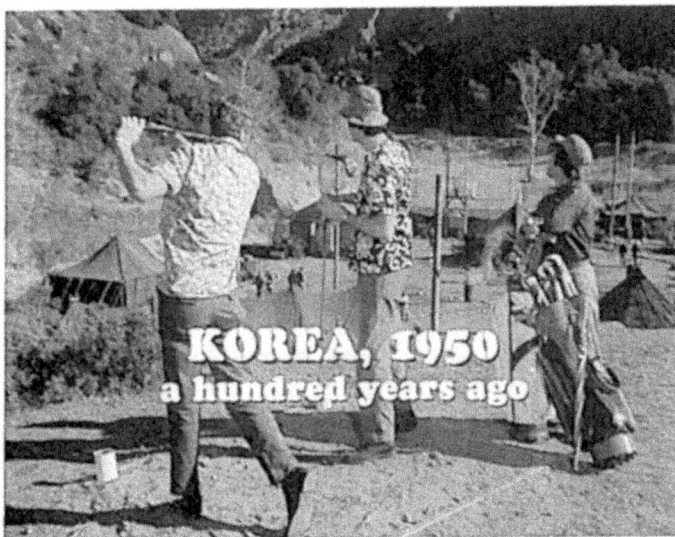

Looking back at the past from the future: time out of joint in the pilot episode

Painless" (minus the lyrics, which can be heard in the film version).[10]

The first two-and-a-half minutes of the pilot episode—a brief, quotidian interlude that leads to an extended version of the now-famous title sequence—encapsulate the thematic and generic contradictions and tensions within the diegetic universe of *M*A*S*H*. Almost every visual element in this pre-credit montage is incongruous, duplicitous, or hybridized. Hawkeye and Trapper are decked out in mismatching flower-print Hawaiian shirts and army green pants. Their golf caddy is the Korean houseboy Ho-jon (played by the Filipino-American actor Patrick Adiarte), and the PA system broadcasts an American song ("My Blue Heaven") but sung in Japanese. Their makeshift "golf course" is simply a rugged hill lined with tents. In place of sand traps is a *real* hazard: a minefield. Apparently scrubbed and dressed for surgery in the OR, Henry and his female companion are not struggling to save a dying patient but rather trying to open a bottle of booze. Margaret and Frank use the pretext of Bible study for an adulterous rendezvous. Father Mulcahy blindly gives out his blessing without actually seeing the object of his consecration. All these events are supposedly happening in Korea in 1950, "a hundred years ago." Given that CBS first broadcast this pilot episode on September 17, 1972 (some twenty-two years after the outbreak of the war), viewers were confronted with the possibility that what they were about to see existed in the realm of fantasy and should not be taken as history. In fact, even today, audiences who watch this first M*A*S*H episode are seeing things from the imaginary vantage point of someone from the future.

The lethargic yet humorous tone of the pre-credits sequence quickly shifts when Radar spots the choppers and the invisible PA announcer summons the medical personnel to report immediately to the operating room. A group of nurses springs into action, dashing from the women's quarters out into the mud. A wet, half-naked man emerges from the shower tent and rushes to answer the call. Another woman hurriedly exits a tent while adjusting her clothing; she is followed by her male partner, who walks away in a different direction, passing a sign that reads "off limits to male personnel." Various leisure and recuperative activities—sports, sex, showering, drinking—all come to an abrupt halt as dedicated medical professionals are called to their duties. We see Hawkeye and Trapper examine wounded soldiers landing from helicopters and give instructions to the support staff. An inserted close-up of Hawkeye's concerned face accentuates the hero's compassionate, caring personality, distinguishing him from his more devil-may-care, cynical predecessors in the original novel and the filmed adaptation.

Immediately following the opening credits, we see Hawkeye in the OR and hear him reciting a letter to his father:

> Dear Dad,
> You said I sounded a bit callous about my job here in my last letter. Well, let me see if I can put it another way. At this particular mobile army hospital, we are not concerned with the ultimate reconstruction of the patient. We only care about getting the kid out of here alive enough for someone else to put on the fine touches. We work fast and we're not dainty because a lot of these kids who can stand two hours on the table just can't stand one second more. We try to play par surgery on this course. Par is a live patient.

This voiceover, which tellingly concludes with a metaphorical reference to golf, centers the male protagonist and immediately forms an emotional bond between him and the viewers. We are privy to his inner thoughts and positioned to lend a sympathetic ear to his plight and frustrations (as his father, a lobster fisherman back home in Crabapple Cove, would no doubt do).

Our medical hero further vocalizes his discontent to Frank when the latter blames him for conduct unbecoming of an officer during the operation: "Frank, I happen to be an officer only because I foolishly opened an invitation from President Truman to come to this costume party. . . . We've all had twelve straight hours of meatball surgery in there! My brain is sending me urgent rest telegrams." However, in the same episode, Hawkeye also experiences a sense of joy and satisfaction when he receives a letter from Dean Lodge, the head of Androscoggin College, informing him that Ho-jon has been accepted to his alma mater. To raise the two thousand dollars needed for the Korean houseboy's tuition and travel expenses, Hawkeye throws an "all-you-can-drink-for-$10" raffle party, offering weekend passes for two to Tokyo as a prize. Radar acquires the passes illegally, hoodwinking Blake into signing them and telling the CO that they are order forms for fudge ripple ice cream. Meanwhile, Hawkeye sweet-talks Lieutenant Maggie Dish (Karen Phillip), an engaged woman whom he has been romancing for weeks, into offering herself as a prize companion for the raffle winner. He also sedates Frank, who has taken temporary command of the unit in Blake's absence, so as to get the meddlesome buffoon out of the way.

The party proves to be a success: over $1,800 is raised and Father Mulcahy—the "resident celibate"—is named the winner because Hawkeye has manipulated the raffle to bail out Lt. Dish.[11] Margaret discovers what has happened to Frank and reports the incident to General Hammond (George Wood), one of her old flames, currently stationed in Seoul. Accompanied by Blake, Hammond quickly descends on the camp, is saluted by Radar (who is wearing a bedpan on his head), breaks up the party, and threatens to court-martial both Hawkeye and Trapper. On cue, incoming wounded Canadian soldiers bring the shindig to a halt and everyone—including Hammond—works together in the OR. Impressed by the two gifted surgeons' knack for stitching up soldiers, the general eventually retracts his order for their arrest. The episode ends with the "meatball surgeons" complaining about their *Catch-22* situation, emphasized when Hawkeye says, "We gotta give up this preoccupation with keeping people alive, or we'll never get outta here. Maybe we should start using rusty instruments." Trapper offers another idea: "Stop washing our hands," to which Hawkeye adds, "Raise our prices!" Following this is a self-reflexive end-credits sequence accompanied by a roll call of the main cast members, spoken by the disembodied male voice of the camp's PA system—something earlier utilized by Altman at the end of his film.

Significantly, this pilot episode reveals a misogynistic streak in the otherwise likeable chief surgeon, who will gradually develop into a more mature and politically conscious character in later seasons of the series, someone who will come to perceive women as well as racial minorities (a group constituting the *majority* in Korea) in an altogether different light. Here, though, Hawkeye rudely addresses Margaret in the OR (who has inquired if everything is okay while wiping sweat from his forehead), telling her, "Yeah, fine. But if you don't move, I'm gonna have to cut around your 'B' cups." When Frank protests against this "unbecoming conduct" after the operation, Hawkeye casually says, "Sorry, baby" to Margaret, who then pulls rank on him and insists "*Major* to you." His sarcastic reply to the outranking female officer: "Sorry, major baby."

Additional hints of Hawkeye's misogyny manifest in his relationship with Lt. Dish, the woman whom he is using as bait in his altruistic raffle. Dish was a creation of Lardner Jr., not Gelbart, and was transported into the television series from Altman's film, where she was little more than an appropriately named object of desire, coerced into sleeping with "Painless" Pole so as to therapeutically remedy his sexual impotency. Not surprisingly, it was this plotline, along with Hot Lips's/Kellerman's humiliation in the film's famous shower scene, that outraged many feminist critics. Ellen Willis, a *Village Voice* columnist, wrote a letter to the *New York Times* denouncing the "blatant misogyny" of Altman's M*A*S*H. Another critic, Sandra Shevey, argued in the same newspaper that the film "obscenely degrades women." Defending his film against these and other feminist accusations, Altman (who never commented on the real-life episode involving an 8076th shower tent that apparently inspired this scene) replied, "This is the way [women] were treated back then (in the 1950s)."[12]

The TV pilot thus dilutes the earlier work's misogyny to a degree, emphasizing that a noble cause (sending a poor Korean boy to college in the United States) is behind Hawkeye's (mis)use of the nurse. As stated earlier, in Hornberger's novel, Hawkeye raises $6,500 for Ho-jon by selling pictures of Trapper John posing as Jesus rather than by compromising a woman's virtue. By the end of the pilot episode, however, Hawkeye has managed to both generate the necessary money *and* prevent Lt. Dish from fulfilling her sexual obligation by secretly instructing the nurse to pick Father Mulcahy's ticket, which has been taped to the bottom of the raffle bowl. The outcome is a surprise even to Lt. Dish, who had earlier anticipated that Hawkeye would doctor the raffle so as to have a shot at her. Despite this gentlemanly gesture, though, Hawkeye doesn't think twice about raffling off the woman he has been romantically pursuing and utters insensitive phrases such as "Hot Lips" and "the completely edible Lieutenant Dish."

Chapter 3

Ensemble TV

As stated in the previous chapter, the pilot episode of *M*A*S*H* aired on September 17, 1972, in the midst of several industrial changes and government rulings designed to bring greater programming diversity to television (these include the Prime-Time Access Rule implemented in 1971 and the FCC-imposed fin-syn rules established the year before, which prevented the big three networks from integrating vertically). When the series premiered, the Columbia Broadcasting System (CBS) had already announced plans to create a separate company for syndication distribution (Viacom), had just shut down its own short-lived film production unit (Cinema Center Films), and had witnessed the retirement of its illustrious radio talk-show host Arthur Godfrey. Its attention now steadfastly focused on television, CBS was experimenting with its schedule and experiencing an upswing in Nielsen ratings, having one year earlier debuted what would become the number one show in America, *All in the Family* (1971–79). This Norman Lear production differs from *M*A*S*H* in many ways, most glaringly in that it was a taped recording of a performance in front of an in-studio audience as opposed to a filmed recording of actors on location or at least partially outside studio walls. Indeed, for all of its groundbreaking use of topical humor in transforming the domestic sitcom into a kind of cultural laboratory for testing socially relevant material (racism, bigotry, sexism, patriarchy, and so forth), *All in the Family*—like two other Lear programs, *Maude* (CBS, 1972–78) and *Sanford and Son* (NBC, 1972–77)—harkens back to earlier examples of live television comedy from the 1950s because of the immediacy and claustrophobia of its soundstage-bound setting.

Although not nearly as "cinematic" as Altman's film, the TV series *M*A*S*H* gave such directors as Hy Averback, Jackie Cooper, Charles Dubin, William Jurgensen, Don Weis, and William Wiard, as well as the screenwriters Larry Balmagia, Jay Folb, Ronny Graham, David Issacs, Allan Katz, Ken Levine, Larry Marks, and Don Reo (among others) the opportunity to incorporate stylistic flourishes and narrative experimentation into several episodes, from fairly elaborate tracking and dolly shots to a ticking clock that counted down, in real time, the minutes needed to perform surgery on a dying soldier (in "Life Time," from season 8). These kinds of techniques and innovations were relatively uncommon during the 1970s (especially so when *M*A*S*H* premiered in the fall of 1972) and are indicative of CBS executives' willingness to take chances on unconventional formats and controversial subject matter.

Although Gelbart claims that he and the other scriptwriters were initially uncertain about the direction the series would take during its first season, noticeable motifs were already beginning to rise to the surface in the first half-dozen episodes, which rely on the following formula: "Hawkeye and Trapper [get] into big trouble (usually followed by a visit from a general)," only to be "exonerated after displaying their vitally necessary talents in the operating room."[1] Spun around this standard narrative setup and resolution are a number of incidental details related to camp life, not to mention several intricately woven narrative threads that suggest a willingness on the part of Gelbart, Metcalfe, and Reynolds to retain Altman's discursive, multidirectional approach to plotting. Indeed, much like the ensemble film, the television series is, in Thomas Schatz's words, "remarkably 'democratic' in its treatment of the eight principal characters," many of whom either take center stage or contribute to the thematic parallelism in subsequent episodes throughout the first season.[2]

Constantly out of uniform and clad in a fishing vest and cap, the TV version of Colonel Henry Blake is presented as a more bumbling, less sober version of the film's camp commander, someone whose proclivity to drink and eagerness to have sex with various women position him as a decidedly non-Army type sympathetic to Hawkeye and Trapper's shenanigans as well as their dislike of Major Frank Burns. Likewise a character retained from both the novel and the film, Burns hails from Fort Wayne, Indiana, and is immediately coded as a jingoistic, xenophobic, anal-retentive, obnoxious, and incompetent doctor, someone who will be repeatedly lampooned by Hawkeye and Trapper for his hypocrisy, pettiness, and pro-military stance. As in the film, the TV version of Burns cheats on his wife with Margaret "Hot Lips" Houlihan, the head nurse at the 4077. Margaret is initially ridiculed because of her steadfast dedication to her military career as well as her romantic association with Burns. Over time, though, she is begrudgingly accepted into Hawkeye and Trapper's exclusive circle, becoming "one of the guys" while at the same time embodying the traits of a strong, independent, career-minded woman.

Each of these characters adds harmonic resonance and texture to the situation-based humor of the first season, which foregrounds the constant oscillation between phenomenological extremes that would distinguish M*A*S*H from all other series on network television during the 1972–73

45

season. In addition to balancing high and low forms of comedy with an emphasis on both verbal and physical humor, M*A*S*H maintains a delicate tonal equilibrium, taking the spectator from the mess tent to the operating room in the blink of an eye. The proximity of these and other radically different spaces marks the show as a workplace comedy quite unlike other famous examples of the genre, such as *The Dick Van Dyke Show* (CBS, 1961–66) and the contemporaneous hit *The Mary Tyler Moore Show* (CBS, 1970–77), both of which depict "co-workers as a loosely knit but crucially interdependent quasi-family within a 'domesticated' workplace."[3]

Whereas these latter programs maintain a physical separation between the workplace that is home to a surrogate family of coworkers and the domestic arena that is home to actual relatives, M*A*S*H literally mashes together these spaces of social interaction so as create greater tension as well as a stronger sense of community in the face of calamity.[4] With sleeping quarters situated next to public showers, with the mess tent doubling as a place of worship,[5] with the OR itself only a short walk from the Officer's Club (which is later renamed the "Henry Blake Memorial Bar" in recognition of his endearing dipsomania), a certain promiscuous blending of genres and genders can be expected, something apparent in the many interactions between so-called soft personnel and the horny doctors who pursue them. Hence the series' focus on sexual flings between the men and women of the 4077, who share their innermost feelings (among other things) in close quarters and come to rely on one another much like actual family members.

Another sign of the blending that results from this spatial collapse or physical proximity is the character of Corporal Maxwell Klinger (Jamie Farr), a cigar-chomping, cross-dressing heterosexual who dons women's clothing in hopes of evading military service and getting a Section Eight from the Army. Nicknamed "Corporal Crazy" because of his desperate, unflagging bid for a mental instability discharge (he even goes so far as to subject his body to physical harm, whether by trying to eat an entire jeep, bit by bit, or by pouring gasoline on himself and threatening to strike a match), Klinger may in fact be the sanest member of the unit, a paradox that fans of Joseph Heller's aforementioned *Catch-22* will certainly grasp given that novel's focus on the many failed attempts by a bomber pilot named Yossarian to avoid dangerous missions by maintaining that he is insane.[6] Like Heller's archetypal World War II antihero, whose claim of insanity does not relieve him from active duty (for what could be saner than wanting to avoid dangerous missions?), Klinger is faced with a seemingly unsolvable dilemma, one that he comically comments on throughout the series: How does one get out of Korea? This lingering conundrum applies not only to Klinger but also to Margaret, Hawkeye, and the only other character to appear in *M*A*S*H* from its first season to its last, Father Francis J. Mulcahy (William Christopher). Likewise similar to a character in *Catch-22* (Chaplain A. T. Tappman, played in the 1970 film by Anthony Perkins, who at one point is referred to as "Padre"), the 4077's quirky man of God watches benevolently over his flock of fellow medicos, seeking solace in the Lord and through restorative letters to his sister, a nun named Kathy (who has adopted the moniker Sister Angelica).

Unlike Father Mulcahy and some of the other people appearing throughout *M*A*S*H*'s first season (including Timothy Brown's "Spearchucker" Jones and John Orchard's "Ugly" John), the character of Klinger was created by Gelbart and is thus not found in either the novel or the film.[7] Debuting in the fourth episode ("Chief Surgeon Who?"), Klinger would soon be joined by other recurring characters written exclusively for the TV series, such as the paranoid CIA operative Colonel Flagg (Edgar Winter), the army psychiatrist Sidney Freedman (Allan Arbus), the dim-witted Private Igor Straminsky (Jeff Maxwell), the supply sergeant Zelmo Zale

47

(Johnny Haymer), and the always dependable half-Hawaiian, half-Chinese nurse Kellye (Kellye Nakahara).[8] As stated earlier, the lone holdover from the film was Gary Burghoff, who reprised his role as "Radar" O'Reilly for the first eight seasons of the television series (until the two-part episode "Goodbye, Radar"). Throughout those years, especially during Colonel Blake's tenure as commanding officer, the eighteen-year-old clairvoyant is an instrumental if mischievous figure in the series—someone who oversees the day-to-day running of the 4077 in his capacity as company clerk yet frequently betrays his innocent, adolescent side while talking to his Teddy Bear, reading Archie comics, or downing shots of Grape Nehi at Rosie's Bar. The hirsute Klinger, a more mature if less responsible character, would eventually take over Radar's post once Burghoff left *M*A*S*H*.

Burghoff was one of four original cast members who departed the series. The other actors to leave—McLean Stevenson, Wayne Rogers, and Larry Linville—were replaced by less acerbic, more likeable performers: Harry Morgan, Mike Farrell, and David Ogden Stiers. Morgan, who had earlier appeared as Major General Steele in the season 3 opener, "The General Flipped at Dawn," was cast as Colonel Sherman T. Potter after Stevenson had decided to exit the series. Stevenson's last appearance as the laid-back Colonel Henry Blake, commanding officer of the 4077, was in the season 3 episode, "Abyssinia, Henry." Written by Jim Fritzell and Everett Greenbaum and originally broadcast on March 18, 1975, this famous episode shocked audiences with the death of Blake, a major character whose tour of duty in Korea had ended (he had accrued enough "points" to go home). It was not, however, the first time that a sympathetic character was killed off in *M*A*S*H*: in season 1, "Sometimes You Hear the Bullet" shows Hawkeye reduced to tears when his childhood friend Tommy Gillis (James Callahan), an author who is writing a firsthand account of infantry life in Korea, perishes as a re-

Corporal "Radar" O'Reilly mourns the loss of Colonel Blake in "Abyssinia, Henry"

sult of gunfire. Still, as moving as this and a handful of other episodes in the first three seasons are, none approach "Abyssinia, Henry" in terms of its unprecedented readiness to kill off a major character for dramatic purposes and emotional effect.

In the closing seconds of this episode, Radar trudges into the operating room holding a telegram and—in one of the most moving and dramatic scenes in the history of *M*A*S*H*—informs everyone that their former CO's homeward bound plane has been shot down over the Sea of Japan. The resulting shock and silence in the OR, broken only by the sharp sound of a scalpel hitting the ground, is rendered as a kind a documentary moment, captured by the camera as it pans across the room and scans the dazed faces of the actors (who were not told about this tragic twist in advance). Besides giving the actor (who was developing *The McLean Stevenson Show* for NBC) a somewhat inglorious sendoff, the show generated a spate of outraged fan mail from viewers who had grown to love the affable yet ineffectual character and felt betrayed by the producers. In the wake of Blake's death, Gelbart, Reynolds, and Metcalfe made significant alterations to the show's formula with the addition of the sixty-two-year-old Colonel Potter, a stern and disciplined yet affectionate taskmaster (not to mention a lover of all things equine) who would eventually become a father figure to many of the younger staff members, particularly Margaret, a character undergoing significant changes around that time.

Another major alteration for the show occurred when Farrell's Captain B. J. Hunnicutt was brought onboard following Wayne Rogers's departure. As Trapper's replacement, the twenty-eight-year-old Hunnicutt, a Stanford graduate, quickly becomes a more wholesome companion to Hawkeye upon his arrival in the season 4 opener, "Welcome to Korea." This change of personnel is thus a change in personality, something subtly connoted by the new character's last name. Whereas Trapper had been a somewhat burly surgeon whose preoccupations included snaring women, Hunnicutt is sweeter, a "cutter" who is like honey compared to his predecessor.[9] A devoted husband and loving father, he embodies a certain set of clearly articulated moral principles from which he rarely deviates. Except for a moment of weakness in "Hanky Panky" (season 5), he remains faithful to his wife throughout his tour of duty. And yet, despite this apparent staunchness on B.J.'s part, he is prone to drink as frequently as Hawkeye and shares with his free-wheeling tent mate a distaste for military regimentation and interoffice bureaucracy, something illustrated in his very first episode.

In the Emmy-winning two-parter "Welcome to Korea," set during September 1952, B.J. gets physically ill after witnessing a soldier's death. However, this inexperienced member of the 4077 quickly learns not only how to cope with his new situation but also how to fit in and gain Hawkeye's respect, first by bellying up to an officer's bar in Kimpo, then by stealing a general's jeep (a throwback to Altman's film), and then, while drunk, by calling Frank—the temporary CO who represents the military mindset at its most corrupt—"ferret face." Nevertheless, the introduction of Hunnicutt as well as the equally monogamous and trustworthy Potter—coming only a few months after Richard Nixon's forced resignation from the presidency on August 9, 1974—signaled the beginning of a transition in the show's treatment of both masculinity and femininity, not to mention a desire in American culture at large to put the nation's inglorious past behind it. Also, as comparatively more straight-laced characters than their hell-raising predecessors, Hunnicutt and Potter personify a populist shift away from the darker themes and satiric bite of the show's first three seasons.

51

The third significant alteration that was made before Radar's departure occurred at the beginning of season 6, in the hour-long episode "Fade Out, Fade In," when Major Charles Emerson Winchester III was ushered in as another comic foil for Hawkeye and B.J. to contend with (in the absence of Burns, who went AWOL after the fifth season, which culminated in Margaret's marriage to Lieutenant Colonel Donald Penobscott). Unlike his more irritating predecessor, David Ogden Stiers's Winchester has been drafted into army service. He is also an accomplished and intelligent surgeon who, over time, grows into a sympathetic figure despite his air of superiority, egotism, and elitism, not to mention his outright bigotry and racism (apparent in such episodes as "Bottle Fatigue," when he objects to his sister's engagement to a "swarthy" Italian; and "Twas the Day after Christmas," when he refers to Klinger, a Lebanese American, as a member of a "lower species").[10]

Having grown up in an affluent Presbyterian neighborhood in Boston (Beacon Hill) and graduated number one in his medical class at Harvard, this New England blueblood embodies the establishment, but in a way that differs from the show's satirical representations of military officials and governmental liaisons. Winchester is the picture of a "cultured" man in the stereotypical sense of the word, an oenophile and a master of bridge so accustomed to sleeping on silk sheets and listening to the orchestral music of Wagner and Mussorgsky (which he prefers to brassy military marches) that he is forced to import these luxuries into Korea. Still, while he may have the hardened emotional shell of a Boston Brahmin, those layers of haughty disdain for the unfortunates below him begin to crack over time, emitting glints of generosity and revealing hints of a more humanitarian side of the character, a development that would have been unthinkable during Frank Burns's tenure. This comes to the fore in a handful of episodes, including "Death Takes a Holiday," a season 9 tearjerker (written and directed by Mike Farrell) in which Charles—upholding a Winchester family tradition—transcends his Scrooge-like persona by anonymously sending candy bars to a nearby orphanage at Christmas. An episode from the final season, "Run for the Money," likewise reveals a sympathetic, melancholic side to the snob, showing Winchester trying to boost the spirits and self-esteem of a soldier who stutters (a speech disorder that Charles's sister, Honoria, also suffers from). He does so by encouraging Private Palmer (Phil Brock) to kick his comic book addiction and try reading great literature (like Melville's *Moby Dick*) for a change—something that many great stutterers throughout history, including Winston Churchill, did.

Major Charles Winchester III and Choi Sung-ho (played by Chinese-American actor Keye Luke) in "Death Takes a Holiday"

Mobility as Metaphor

By the end of its first season, when it had been shown opposite such long-running Sunday night programs as *The Wonderful World of Disney* (a.k.a. *Disneyland,* NBC, 1955–90) and *The FBI* (ABC, 1965–74), *M*A*S*H* ranked forty-sixth in the Nielsen ratings. Although not an immediate success, the CBS series dodged cancellation after its first dismal season and managed to become a hit from its second season onward, thanks primarily to a shuffling of the network's schedule (it was moved to a powerhouse Saturday evening slot between *All in the Family* and *The Mary Tyler Moore Show*). Even after its third-season move to Tuesday nights, *M*A*S*H* continued to draw large audiences. Larry Gelbart left the production at the end of the fourth season (1975–76), after having written what is generally considered to be the best episode in the program's history, "The Interview" (a black-and-white mock documentary that I discuss in chapter 7). Gene Reynolds followed suit a year later, so as to devote time to *Lou Grant* (CBS, 1977–82), a spin-off of the MTM Productions flagship series *The Mary Tyler Moore Show.* Although he stayed on as a creative consultant throughout the remaining seasons of *M*A*S*H*, Reynolds was replaced by Burt Metcalfe, who took over as executive producer during this transitional period. Besides producing the series from the sixth season onward, Metcalfe also directed over two-dozen episodes, three of which ("Bottle Fatigue," "No Laughing Matter," and "Picture This") would be nominated for Emmy Awards. Although his contributions to the show have sometimes been ignored in favor of his more famous partners, Metcalfe was the only scriptwriter and producer to work throughout the entire run of the series.[1]

As its fifth season (1976–77) was drawing to a close, M*A*S*H was among the most watched American television shows, landing in the top ten Nielsen-rated programs each year thereafter until the very end.[2] Throughout these later years, when CBS made one final scheduling adjustment

(moving M*A*S*H from Tuesday to Monday nights at 9:00 p.m., beginning with the episode "The Smell of Music"), the series weathered writers' strikes (during its ninth season) and key personnel changes behind the scenes. Still, the show's core group of writers remained at the top of its form, building elaborate scaffolding for the rich linguistic tapestries that were being so effortlessly woven by Alda and the rest of the cast each week. However, the protagonists' innuendo-sprinkled banter was also laced with sanctimonious, self-righteous platitudes about the senselessness of war. This, plus the show's gradual abandonment of overtly antiauthoritarian themes, became the focus of critics who lamented its apparent drop in quality and its retreat to more conservative—or at least populist—sociopolitical territory.

Indeed, in the season 11 episode "Bombshells," a guilt-ridden B.J. utters a statement epitomizing the shift in tone and sentiment that distinguishes the show's final two seasons from its first two. After enemy gunfire forces him to abandon an injured soldier in the field, B.J. returns to the Swamp in a disconsolate state and tells Hawkeye, "We sit around here in our Hawaiian shirts and red suspenders, thumbing our nose at the army, drinking home-brewed gin and flaunting authority at every turn and feeling oh-so-superior to those military fools who kill each other and oh-so-self-righteous when we clean up after them. Well, good luck to you, pal. I hope you can keep it up." By the time this episode aired on November 28, 1982, *M*A*S*H* had already witnessed a noticeable shift in producer Metcalfe's priorities. While each of the show's main characters had developed into a complex individual whose personal conflicts proved more timeless than those witnessed in the more topical sitcom *All in the Family,* one could not help but detect significant season-to-season changes, which in hindsight clearly reflect political, social, and institutional transformations in the United States.

In one of the show's many epistolary narratives, "Dear Sis" (from season 7), Father Mulcahy writes in closing to his sister Kathy, "You know, sis, it doesn't matter whether you feel useful or not when you're moving from one disaster to another. The trick, I guess, is just to keep moving." This comment, which leads to a rare freeze-frame that caps the episode with an image of combined movement and stasis, is meant to denote the chaplain's change of heart: he has cathartically overcome his feelings of guilt (after punching an injured soldier) and worthlessness (as a spiritual guide rather than a physical healer) during the camp's Christmas celebration. However, one could just as easily read Mulcahy's allusion to movement as a reference to the idea that recurring characters in long-running television programs inevitably undergo changes of some sort. This was especially true of *M*A*S*H,* which indeed went through significant alterations over the course of several years, humanizing Houlihan, heteronormativizing Klinger, and heroicizing Hawkeye's newfound ability (or willingness) to treat women with respect.

The show's many diegetic modifications (which reflect shifts in societal attitudes as well as changes in America's political climate), not to mention the extradiegetic flux involved in the hiring of new actors, are in contrast to the characters' inability to escape war-torn Korea. Hence the paradox of having characters who are both immobile (confined to the same setting, except in those rare "bug outs" brought about by heavy enemy fire) and mobile (shifting allegiances, personalities, and behavioral patterns as part of a maturation process). Set against the same nondescript backdrop of mountains week-to-week and featuring a seemingly endless litany of incoming wounded in addition to the show's familiar faces, M*A*S*H nevertheless adopted Mulcahy's modus operandi: it just kept moving. In doing so, it managed to continuously move audiences who stuck with the program long enough to witness emotionally satisfying developments (like Margaret's "gradual transition from sex object-martinet to sympathetic woman") as well as a more general shift to introspection, which, as Elisabeth Weis points out, "paralleled the increased self-examination and narcissism of the early eighties."[3]

Perhaps the most moving episode of M*A*S*H was the final one. Clocking in at an unprecedented two-and-a-half hours, "Goodbye, Farewell, and Amen" might just as easily have been titled "The Long Goodbye" given its extended series of scenes in which cast members depart by jeep, truck, and helicopter during the last thirty minutes, bidding their adieus to other cast members as well as to the audience, the largest ever to watch a single television episode in the medium's history. Leading up to those scenes, though, is a string of compelling subplots involving all of the main characters, including Klinger (who has fallen in love with Soon-lee, a Korean woman searching for her parents), Charles (who is teaching a quartet of Chinese musicians how to play Mozart), and Father Mulcahy (who loses his hearing while trying to free prisoners in the midst of heavy shelling). These parallel storylines, which play out in anticipation of an armistice agreement that will bring the war to a halt, are juxtaposed with scenes of a traumatized Hawkeye receiving psychiatric care from Sidney Freedman in a hospital somewhere in Korea.

Aired on February 28, 1983 (roughly thirty years after the 1953 armistice was signed), and watched by a record-setting 106 million viewers (in over 50 million households nationwide), this tearjerker of a finale stands as a testament to the widespread appeal of M*A*S*H, a Korean War dramedy that—although set in the late Truman, early Eisenhower era—reflected contemporaneous attitudes about pressing social concerns from the last days of the Nixon administration to the first years of the Reagan administration. Is it merely coincidental that the abovementioned first-season episode "Sometimes You Hear the Bullet," which marked a shift from rib-tickling comedy to tear-inducing tragedy, was broadcast on January 28, 1973, almost exactly ten years before the series finale and just one day after President Richard Nixon had appeared on television announcing the peace treaty that would end the Vietnam War? The fact that "Goodbye, Farewell, and Amen" was broadcast only four months after the Vietnam Veterans Memorial designed by Maya Lin was opened to the public (on November 13, 1982) feeds into the critical consensus positing M*A*S*H as a metaphorical statement about "the denial of America's role" in that particular war. The historian James H. Wittebols makes an excellent case for such a reading, pointing out that the primary storyline in the final episode, which "focuses on Hawkeye's recognition of and recovery from the trauma he suffered when he held himself responsible for the woman suffocating her crying baby," hinges on the suppression of a memory and—by extension—a denial of the past.[4]

Several other episodes, such as "For the Good of the Outfit" and "As You Were" (season 2 episodes that deal with "friendly fire" incidents linked to the U.S. military's use of napalm) and "Mad Dogs and Servicemen" (a season 3 episode that indirectly alludes to Vietnam as "the next war"), support

Wittebols's argument. However, as acceptable as that reading is, to put so much emphasis on M*A*S*H's allegorical relationship to the Vietnam War is to perhaps deny its significance as a television series concerned first and foremost with the Korean War, which has been referred to as "The Forgotten War" in American popular culture. Although many critics have argued persuasively that in its later seasons the emphasis of the show shifted from the political to the interpersonal, taking the audience further away from the historical context of the war, I argue that, while character rather than situation became increasingly important, the unique *setting* of the series—Korea—continued to dominate and shape the experiences of the doctors and nurses until its final episode, which not coincidentally features a wedding between the Lebanese American Klinger and the Korean Soon-lee.

A true cultural event, the final episode of M*A*S*H ranks alongside the miniseries *Roots* (ABC, 1977), the season opener of the "Who Shot J.R.?" episode of *Dallas* (CBS, 1978–91), and some of the most-watched Super Bowl games as an object of mass appeal, "authenticating the metaphors of television as a national hearth or a global village."[5] "Goodbye, Farewell, and Amen" might appear to have signaled the demise of the Korean War genre in American popular culture, and yet television shows of the 1980s and 1990s continued to feature Korean War veterans as main or secondary characters, such as Philip Drummond (Conrad Bain) in *Diff'rent Strokes* (NBC, 1978–76), Benson DuBois (Robert Guillaume) in *Benson* (ABC, 1979–86), Frank Costanza (Jerry Stiller) in *Seinfeld* (NBC, 1989–98), Maurice J. Minnifield (Barry Corbin) in *Northern Exposure* (CBS, 1990–95), Martin Crane (John Mahoney) in *Frasier* (NBC, 1993–2004), George Carey (Stanley Anderson) in *The Drew Carey Show* (ABC, 1995–2004), Red Forman (Kurtwood Smith) in *That '70s Show* (Fox, 1998–2006), and Harold Weir (Joe Flaherty) in *Freaks and*

Geeks (ABC, 1999–2000). However, while a couple of the abovementioned series, not to mention several episodes of *M*A*S*H* (including "Aid Station," "The Chosen People," "The General's Practitioner," and "Ain't Love Grand"), deal with interracial marriage and romance between Americans and Koreans, only *AfterMASH* (CBS, 1983–84), the spin-off to *M*A*S*H*, explores the deep-seated prejudices that war brides encountered upon arrival in the United States. I shall return to *AfterMASH*, a critically disparaged series deserving of reevaluation, as well as the aforementioned "Goodbye, Farewell, and Amen," at the end of this book.[6]

"Dead Serious" in Living Color

Although, as Donald McBride argues, television coverage of the Korean War "was sketchy at best" during the years in which it was fought (1950–53), this "police action" was nevertheless brought to the attention of the American public through other media, entertainment, and news outlets.[1] Beginning in January 1951, William Gaines's EC comic book series *Two-Fisted Tales* offered visceral, blood-soaked depictions of the fighting presented in bold primary colors that contributed to its combined realism and artifice. On the first day of that same month, *Time* featured a "Man of the Year" cover spread in which a composite image and profile of the American fighting man provided readers a glimpse into the military mindset.[2]

A few other cultural productions of the early 1950s served a significant role in educating the populace about the events in Korea. One notable example came from the photojournalist David Douglas Duncan, a contributor to *Life* magazine who landed with General Douglas MacArthur and the X Corps at Inch'ŏn in September 1950. Duncan's pictures of "The Big Mac" (as he is sometimes referred to in *M*A*S*H*) would be disseminated in the media for years to come, capturing heroic images of the Supreme Commander of U.N. Forces as he drove the marines up to the Chosin Reservoir. Accompanying Duncan on that historical Inch'ŏn landing and northward drive was the Pulitzer Prize–winning war correspondent Marguerite Higgins, author of the best-selling book *War in Korea* (1951), which likewise bolstered popular opinion and support for the war "as a necessary effort to contain the expansion of international communism."[3] Once the Chinese People's Liberation Army crossed the Yalu River and sent American and other U.N. troops retreating, stateside support for the war dropped off precipitously, and news coverage of the conflict was eventually pushed to the periphery as it stretched on through several armistice negotiations.

At first, the Korean War was seen by Hollywood executives as the means for a possible return to the economic prosperity that the studios had enjoyed during World War II, something of paramount importance given the increasingly competitive atmosphere in which TV—a new medium—was threatening the old system's hegemony by luring audiences away from movie theaters. But for all their initial optimism, this ultimately unpopular war proved to be less than lucrative for the production and distribution companies involved. To their credit, major studios like Twentieth Century-Fox and Warner Bros. tentatively released a few independently produced, low-budget films from mavericks like Samuel Fuller (*The Steel Helmet* [1951], *Fixed Bayonets* [1951]) and Joseph H. Lewis (*Retreat, Hell!* [1952]), which feature harrowing depictions of American soldiers suffering psychological crises and physical injuries, not to mention inglorious defeats that were anathema to audiences familiar with earlier biopics and war epics like *Sergeant York* (1941), *Pride of the Marines* (1945), and *The Sands of Iwo Jima* (1949). But these and other representative Korean War films, such as *Battle Circus* (1953), *Flight Nurse* (1953), *The Glory Brigade* (1953), and *Over Korea* (1953), failed to resonate with mainstream moviegoers. Even the "prestige" and "A" pictures produced by Hollywood studios after the 1953 ceasefire, including *The Bridges at Toko-Ri* (1955), *The McConnell Story* (1955), *The Hunters* (1958), and *Cry for Happy* (1961), tended to abstract or generalize the Korean War rather than deal with specific combat-related areas or events,[4] treating the conflict as an ideological showdown between the United States and the Communist forces of the Soviet Union and Red China rather than a fratricidal conflict that cost over one million Korean lives.

While Fuller's *The Steel Helmet* (shot in a mere twelve days in and around Ventura Hills) and a handful of other independent and studio-produced narrative films offer documentary-like moments that transport the viewer into perilous settings, only one motion picture produced during the war—John Ford's *This Is Korea!* (1951)—brims with the kind of verisimilitude that could only otherwise be found in archival documents. The "reality effect" of this hour-long documentary derives less from the offscreen narrator's incessant reminders that "this is Korea" than from its footage of actual combat maneuvers with mortars and rockets firing incessantly over Korean mountainsides, not to mention its handheld camerawork and spectacular color cinematography. As a testament to this film's historical significance, many of the network news broadcasts that reported the war simply recycled footage from *This Is Korea!* and "relied almost exclusively on . . . copy furnished by the armed forces" to describe what was happening in the war.[5] One notable exception to this was CBS's *See It Now* (1951–58), an award-winning program produced by Edward R. Murrow and Fred Friendly that—among other things—exposed the hypocrisies of McCarthy-era America and revealed the quiz show scandals that rocked the burgeoning television industry. One of the most popular episodes of *See It Now*, "Christmas in Korea," showed Murrow interviewing American soldiers stationed throughout the snow-covered peninsula in 1952, speaking not to high-ranking officials but rather to the grunts on the ground doing "the dirty work." This personal approach to telling the soldiers' stories, in addition to one interviewee's comment that the war was "a bunch of nonsense," later informed Larry Gelbart's screenplay for "The Interview."[6]

"The Interview" aired on February 24, 1976, marking Gelbart's last contribution to the series before his departure at the end of season 4. This famous black-and-white chamber-drama, involving the arrival of a news correspondent (Clete Roberts, playing himself) who conducts interviews with Hawkeye, B.J., Father Mulcahy, Frank, Radar, Klinger, and Colonel Potter, was one of the few episodes to be aired by CBS without a laugh track and is notable for the cast members' improvised reactions to the journalist's questions about war, death, fear, work, boredom, camaraderie, and their plans for the future.[7] "The Interview" self-reflexively begins with an offscreen announcer stating the obvious: that this is a black-and-white episode. Microphone in hand, Roberts directly addresses the camera while standing in the OR, explaining how the concept of a mobile army surgical hospital is being tested in Korea and how it has generated a 97 percent effectiveness rating. He then promises to introduce us to the people behind "that most impressive statistic," turning first to Hawkeye, whose talking-head interview begins with another self-reflexive comment from the announcer: "Some of their saltier comments have been deleted." The occasional "bleeps" that mask such expletives as "ass," "shit," and "son of a bitch" are as startling as the many jump cuts utilized throughout this quickly edited, deadly serious drama wherein Hawkeye admits to being so afraid at times that his cot shakes from the pounding of his heart.

In conventional military documentary mode, every interviewee is subsequently introduced by subtitles indicating name and rank. However, most of the men's responses are anything but conventional. Hawkeye claims to specialize in

Clete Roberts as a news correspondent in "The Interview"

boredom, something exacerbated by the monotony of the surroundings and the omnipresence of green (a color that is associated with the military and, in the episode "Peace on Us," is replaced by red as the men and women dye everything—including their clothing and hair—deep crimson in hopes of alleviating the surgeon's ennui).[8] He then jokes about having written a heartfelt letter to Elizabeth Truman, and then breaks into his routine antiwar wisecracks before the camera. His interview is interrupted by several other talking-head segments, with B.J. describing his multitasking duties ("anesthesiologist one day, orthopedist the next, psychologist pretty much all the time"); Radar talking about racing earthworms and cockroaches; Frank naming Korea as a "shining example of the American policy of benign military intervention"; Klinger complaining about the misnomer "police action" for a full-fledged war; Potter praising the virtues of Abraham Lincoln, who is compared to Harry Truman; and Father Mulcahy describing the steam that rises from open bodies during winter, when doctors are forced to warm themselves over the gaping wounds.

The conspicuous absence of Margaret (or any other nurse) as an interviewee is remedied to a certain degree in another macabre example of mockumentary reportage—the season 7 episode "Our Finest Hour." This hour-long episode, shown in two parts after the series was syndicated, features many of the same elements found in "The Interview," including black-and-white cinematography and improvisational responses to the questions of Clete Roberts, who again plays himself (a news correspondent in the Korean War). Once more, all of the main male characters answer queries about what they miss most from the United States (B.J., now with mustache, says that he yearns for his wife's cooking). However, while "Hot Lips" remains offscreen in the former episode, "Our Finest Hour" brings her front and center, at least for a portion of the diegesis, which makes a strong case for the diversity of the camp's medical personnel, who have nevertheless overcome their differences to become, in her words, "a family."

The title—"Our Finest Hour"—is ironic given the fact that the words recall Winston Churchill's famous speech of June 18, 1940 (after Nazi Germany had attacked Britain), and because the interviewees in this episode complain about bad food, intolerable heat and cold, and lack of privacy. Still, as a reflexive comment from the show's producers, who were seeking to showcase some of the funniest and most moving segments from previous episodes, the title is fitting. Recontextualized in a sixty-minute clipfest interspersed with archival images from Movietone newsreels (showing 1950s icons such as Queen Elizabeth, Marilyn Monroe, Joe DiMaggio, and Joseph McCarthy plus documentary footage of the actual Korean War), as well as newly shot black-and-white mockumentary interviews, these color segments take on a new meaning. Spectatorial pleasure plays into the meaningfulness of "Our Finest Hour" insofar as audiences are invited to identify the many embedded clips drawn from such episodes as "Adam's Rib," "Hanky Panky," "Change of Command," "Comrades in Arms," "Crisis," "The Nurses," and "Abyssinia Henry." A question asked by Potter early in this unusual episode—"Which war is this?" (the same question asked by the titular surgeon in "Hawkeye Get Your Gun")—reflects not only the interchangeability of military experiences for the "regular army" colonel who previously served in World Wars I and II but also the interepisodic slippage that occurs when so many clips (including scenes from "The Interview") are placed back-to-back. Despite offering very little in the way of new material, this episode is notable for the way it collapses time and space, bringing together Lt. Col. Blake and his replacement Col. Potter as well as B.J. and his predecessor Trapper. Burns, he of the flared nostrils and weaselly demeanor, is once again featured (only in clips this time), as is his successor, Winchester, someone about whom Father Mulcahy struggles to say anything nice.

The slippages don't end there, though. The temporal setting within the diegesis (October 9, 1952) mirrors the original airdate of the episode (October 9, 1978). The spatial settings likewise bleed into one another, with Clete Roberts not only speaking from the recovery room (and alluding to his previous visit to the 4077, since which virtually no dramaturgical time has passed) but also interviewing his subjects from the mess tent, sleeping quarters, and—in the episode's most significant break from "The Interview"—operating room. Newly shot footage sits side by side with previously recorded material, much of which comes from the first three seasons, before the departures of Trapper and Blake. Truman, Eisenhower, and Nixon are all shown speaking to their delegates in documentary newsreels, which lend a hint of irony to the surrounding scenes of horseplay (described by B.J. as "clean American fun").

Roberts's early comment that an end to the Korean War "seems nowhere in sight" might well be a self-reflexive gesture about the longevity of M*A*S*H, just as Radar's complaint about the way "people come and go around here" might be construed as an allegorical response to the show's many cast changes. "You just get to know one person and he leaves, and then there's another person," the company clerk states in a scene that not coincidentally cuts to Trapper John preparing to go AWOL. Attempting to dissuade his pal from resorting to so extreme a measure, Hawkeye says, "You gotta stick around and see how it ends," to which Trapper responds, "Oh, but it doesn't end, it's continuous. When it finishes here, they take it on the road." This response, which echoes a similar statement from Hawkeye in "Peace on Us" (he complains "It's never gonna stop!" after the P'anmunjom peace talks break down), slyly refers to the fact that M*A*S*H—like the Korean War—never really ended; that syndication took the series beyond its official termination.[9]

At one point in "Our Finest Hour" Clete Roberts says, "If you were going to hold a war, this is probably the most brutal climate on Earth in which to do it." While this might be an exaggeration, it is true that the weather conditions endured by the men and women of the real MASH units during the Korean War were often severe. These extremes are shown in such episodes as "Crisis" and "It Happened One Night," in which the 4077 fends off cold winds while Klinger—itching to escape Korea—does his best to get frostbite, going so far as to strip down to his skivvies. In M*A*S*H, such conditions are meteorological manifestations of the deeper, psychological scars with which the soldiers, doctors, and nurses were dealing.

Two episodes from season 7 deserve mention here for the way they bring together, in the space of just one week, radically dissimilar situations. Originally broadcast on October 23, 1978, "None Like It Hot" finds the 4077 in the midst of a heat wave, with temperatures soaring to 104 degrees Fahrenheit. In an effort to assuage their misery, Hawkeye and B.J. have ordered a portable canvas bathtub from Abercrombie and Fitch, which arrives just in time for them and the entire camp (including Klinger, who—dressed in a sweatsuit and fur coat—smells like "a dead raccoon" and "a garlic blossom") to partake in its restorative power. Oddly, this episode was followed the next week by "They Call the Wind Korea." Airing on October 30, it concerns a very different meteorological condition, with strong storms originating in Manchuria blowing cold winds into the camp, thus ruining Winchester's planned trip to Tokyo for R & R. When seen back-to-back, these two episodes reveal the extreme conditions in Korea and highlight the series' ability to swerve wildly from one environmental and psychological state to another. And just as major weather changes frequently set off explosives near the camp (see, for instance, "Deluge" and "Baby It's Cold Outside"), so too do the doctors and nurses go ballistic at times when rain, sleet, ice, or snow interferes with their medical duties and prevents them from doing the things they most want to do.

Featuring intimate scenes between doctors and nurses that could not have been captured by Clete Roberts's camera crew, "Our Finest Hour" seems somewhat contrived as an excuse to situate footage from earlier episodes within a mock documentary frame. However, the season 9 episode "War for All Seasons" is comparatively successful as a "clip show." The half-hour episode's premise would have us believe that we are watching an entire year's worth of events, from one New Year's Eve celebration to the next. Lacking the flashback structure of the "letter home" episodes like "Dear Dad," this ambitious attempt to telescope so much diegetic time finds the 4077 at once looking back on the previous year's proceedings and anticipating what will transpire in the months ahead. Thankfully, the screenwriters, Dan Wilcox and Thad Mumford, sprinkle in just enough clues to gauge the temporal shifts from season to season. For instance, we witness Father Mulcahy's newly planted flower and vegetable garden grow in the summer only to wither in the winter. Margaret knits a small potholder that likewise develops into something bigger: a scarf and then a sweater. B.J. and Hawkeye's efforts to make a kidney machine from scratch (with parts ordered from a Sears Roebuck catalog) parallel the camp's interest in the professional baseball season back home, one that ends with the Giants winning the pennant. When a 16mm film of that historic game is shown in the mess tent, Charles (who lost lots of money in the betting pool) rushes toward the movie screen and slashes it with a knife—a violent gesture that not only indicates just how angry the major is but also illustrates the emotional extremes produced by this powerful medium.

The aforementioned episodes were not the first to feature black-and-white interviews with the main characters. As early as the season 1 episode "Yankee Doodle Doctor," the series' creators were examining the relationship between television and film, fiction and reality, dramatic reenactments and direct address. Here, the 4077 is handpicked by General Crandall Clayton (Herb Voland) to be the subject of a new military documentary. He dispatches Lieutenant Bricker (Ed Flanders), the film's director, to the camp where it will be shot, the latter offering Hawkeye the starring role, "Yankee Doodle Doctor." Fed up with the propagandistic content of Bricker's work, Trapper and Hawkeye expose the negative—thus ruining the movie—and make their own opus instead. With General Clayton in attendance, the newly shot film is screened in the mess tent. This embedded short, like a mise en abyme, is an unorthodox black comedy featuring Hawkeye and Trapper as anarchic quacks dressed like Groucho and Harpo Marx. In one scene, Hawkeye pours champagne into a woman's shoe and declares, "I give you the war." The rest of the 4077 staff follows suit, drinking from their own shoes before collectively yelling "Yuck!"

Tonally, things take a turn by the end of their film. Hawkeye directly addresses the camera while sitting beside a patient who has a 50/50 chance of survival, saying, "We win some, we lose some. That's what it's all about. No promises. No guaranteed survival. No saints in surgical garb. Our willingness, our experience, our technique are not enough. Guns and bombs and antipersonnel mines have more power to take life than we have to preserve it. Not a very happy ending for a movie. But then, no war is a movie." The screen-within-the screen fades out with a long shot of Hawkeye making a round in post-op. Like M*A*S*H itself, "Yankee Doodle Doctor" is a fascinating, contradictory text that is at once upbeat and downbeat. It continually oscillates between satire and mockumentary, frivolity and tragedy. As the camera cuts to a reaction shot of the viewers in attendance, the general appears dissatisfied. He orders that all the comic business between his patriotic, talking-head introduction (shot by Bricker in propaganda mode) and Hawkeye's final direct address be cut out before any others see it. Nevertheless, Clayton orders that one uncut copy be put aside for his own private viewing, thus recognizing the comedic and—by extension—cathartic roles such cultural productions play.

Hot Lips, Hostilities,
and the Cold War of the Sexes

Hawkeye: "What do you want from me?"

Houlihan: "Respect!"

> *A pivotal exchange in the season 5
> episode "Hepatitis"*

Thus far, I have explored the production background of
M*A*S*H as well as its connection to literary and filmic
antecedents, not to mention similar TV shows from the
1970s that challenged, in some way, the status quo. The final
three chapters map out the complex and evolving relationships of the men and women in the 4077, moving from an
examination of the interrelated issues of sex, gender, and
identity to a discussion of racial representations and the politics of place. In addition to exploring the significance of
Korea as both a real space and an imaginary geography in
M*A*S*H, I wish to turn the spotlight on the one individual
who was most central to the series' success. Indeed, given his
importance to the program, it is imperative that we consider
the issues of gender, sexuality, and identity through the lens
of Alan Alda's onscreen and offscreen personalities, which
contradict yet inform one another and provide a compelling

snapshot of the cultural norms and social patterns that characterized the 1970s and early 1980s. Before focusing on Alda's Hawkeye in chapter 7, I wish to turn the spotlight on another equally important character: head nurse Margaret Houlihan.

As played by Loretta Swit, Margaret in some ways embodies the split image of white American femininity during the 1950s, a polarized image symbolized by two popular Hollywood stars of the era: Marilyn Monroe, whose untamed sexual energy was tempered by vulnerability and a worshipful relationship to men; and Doris Day, whose fresh-faced, girl-next-door demeanor suggested all-American wholesomeness at a time when middle-class families were adopting suburban lifestyles. Houlihan's nickname—"Hot Lips"—suggests sexual experience and indicates her centrality to (hetero)sexist discourses that posit her and many other female characters as little more than passive objects of the male gaze. However, Houlihan's dual drives to faithfully abide by army regulations and to enjoy flirtatious affairs with high-ranking officers, which bespeak an apparent rift between professional goals and personal desires, problematize any attempts to pin her to a fixed stereotype. Her initial dedication to the man she marries at the end of season 5 (the philandering Colonel Donald Penobscot, whom she later divorces) might be read as an extension, or internalization, of her commitment to the military. Indeed, at one point in the season 3 episode "Aid Station," she tells Major Burns, "I'm a married man, too, Frank—married to the Army."

Nevertheless, one cannot ignore the fact that this strong yet vulnerable, callous yet sensitive, uptight yet passionate career woman (who, in her own words, was "born to serve") goes through significant changes throughout the series, which not coincidentally debuted the same year that the Equal Rights Amendment (ERA) was passed by Congress (in 1972, before being sent to the states for ratification) and ended around the time the amendment died (in 1983, after failing to achieve ratification in many states). The ERA, which grew out of the suffragette movement and the National Women's Party of the 1920s, had actually reached the Senate in 1950, the same year the Korean War began. That was just one year after Simone de Beauvoir wrote her feminist classic *Le Deuxième Sexe* (1949), a text originally printed in French and then translated, four years later (in 1953, the year the Korean War ended), into English. A famous quote from *The Second Sex*—"One is not born, but rather becomes, a woman"—puts forth the idea that femininity is not a changeless essence but rather a *process* mired in the sociopolitical conditions of particular eras. Broadcast during the height of the women's liberation movement and coinciding with the emergence of "radicalized" feminism, *M*A*S*H* registers the shifting, often contradictory cultural perceptions of the "Second Sex"—attitudes that are themselves indicative of the mainstream American public's ambivalence about the role of women in the military during the 1970s and 1980s.

Margaret's exhortation—"Don't think of me as a woman" (in the episode "Aid Station")—not only complicates the claim that her character serves as a symbol of the feminist movement (evolving into a more humanized portrait of non-gender-specific independence) but also forces us to acknowledge the series' privileging of patriarchal figures, particularly Colonel Sherman Potter, whom she looks up to as a paternal surrogate and abiding source of strength. Having served in two previous world wars and recently inherited Colonel Blake's post as commanding officer after the latter's tragic death, Potter proves to be a significantly different CO than his bumbling predecessor, whose unique brand of "leadershipmanship" (to borrow Henry's own mangled phrase) and proclivity to flirt with the nurses put him in league with the other rogues of the show, Hawkeye and Trapper.

Potter, while sympathetic to Hawkeye's, Trapper's, and

(later) B.J.'s shenanigans as well as their reasonable dislike of Burns, frequently attempts to keep these potentially anarchic figures in check, and—as a longtime army man—has apparently seen it all. Upon his arrival to the camp in the season 4 episode "Change of Command," Potter does not blink an eye when he first meets Corporal Max Klinger, the latter clad in a garish dress. Perhaps this is because Potter too is in touch with his "feminine" side, something suggested in the season 7 episode "The Price," where we learn that—behind his hard exterior, beneath his uniform—the commanding officer wears pink silk boxers.

As an exemplar of moral uprightness, Colonel Potter even risks slipping from his esteemed position by flirting with members of the opposite sex on a couple of occasions, as shown in the episodes "Lil" and "That's Show Biz," the former featuring Carman Matthews as a visiting nurse who is Sherman's age and the latter a two-parter with a fifty-something ex-stripper named Brandi Doyle (Gwen Verdon) touring Korea with a group of USO performers. Significantly, it is Brandi—the one who presents a challenge to Sherman's monogamy—who vocally acknowledges the communal ethos of the camp, saying to Margaret, "They're like your family."

If there is one persistent motif throughout the later seasons of the series, it is the familial nature of this group of disparate individuals. At the head of this "family" is Potter, who on many occasions is forced to treat the men and women of the 4077 like boys and girls (as, for instance, in "Commander Pierce," when he tells a temporarily "broken-up" Hawkeye and Hunnicutt to shake hands and drink in a gesture of goodwill; or in "Father's Day," when he has to step in after Margaret's own father, Al "Howitzer" Houlihan, has failed in his parenting duties).[1] Ironically, only after Potter assumes command does Margaret begin to soften her regular army rhetoric, take a husband, quickly divorce, and forge a stronger, more sympathetic relationship with the other nurses as well as with Hawkeye—the bickering "brother" to her "sister" in this surrogate family of sorts.

The season 5 episode "Bug Out" is one of the major moments in the series signaling a shift in the rocky relationship between Hawkeye and Margaret. With Chinese troops closing in, the 4077 receives an order from headquarters to uproot tent poles and pull out from what will soon become a war zone. Hawkeye has just performed a laminectomy on a young solider whose spinal cord has been damaged. Since the patient cannot be moved until twenty-four hours after the operation, Hawkeye volunteers to stay behind to look after him in the empty hospital. To his surprise, Margaret, who assisted him in the operation, insists on remaining there as well. Hawkeye awkwardly jokes about her ulterior motives, saying, "You finally realize I have a beautiful body." Margaret puts the freeze on this sexual innuendo and firmly draws a professional line, replying "Let's keep our relationship medical."

Like a combative couple in a classic screwball comedy, Margaret and Hawkeye walk an emotional tightrope, constantly oscillating between physical attraction and professed repulsion, collegial loyalty and jocular animosity, mild flirtations and outright confrontations. The two stranded individuals, bound by dedication to their patient and fear of the incoming enemy, share a brief yet touching moment of commiseration after the other medical personnel (with the exception of Radar) have bugged out. Against the sonic backdrop of artillery fire, Margaret confesses her dread of a "fate worse than death," asking, "Does the enemy rape female prisoners?" Departing from his usual cynicism and nonchalance, Hawkeye assures her, "Margaret, there's no reason to be afraid." However, he quickly confides his own fear, adding, "The minute this kid is stable and on the chopper, I may wet my pants and suck my thumb"—a comment that recalls his confession in an earlier episode dealing with the threat of imminent death that his "whole body is one white knuckle." Thus, Hawkeye inhabits a slippery masculine subject position, which compels him to act vigilant in protecting the chastity of the white woman from the offscreen "yellow horde" despite the fact that he has neither the physical prowess nor the macho gusto to do so.

The next morning, after the patient gets safely flown out by helicopter, Hawkeye, Radar, and Margaret look around the now-empty grounds of the 4077, feeling nostalgic and melancholic. When Radar comments, "Just think of all the guys we operated on," Hawkeye remarks with a touch of remorse, "A lot of them didn't make it." Margaret does her best to bolster his spirits, saying, "Most of them did. You should be proud." Hawkeye reciprocates her support by saying, "You too," and kissing her gently on the cheek. This tender gesture accentuates their increased mutual respect for one another (despite the ongoing verbal quarrels in subsequent episodes). As Hawkeye and his company are about to evacuate in a jeep, they suddenly panic upon hearing the sound of vehicles approaching from afar. Margaret once again expresses her racialized fear of sexual violation: "I'm going to be ravaged! I know it!" Hawkeye grudgingly reassures her in an ironic tone, "Tell 'em you're with me," betraying his own masculine anxiety. The trio frantically circles around the wooden structures of the 4077 tents in a vain attempt to escape the enemy only to find out that it is their own returning staff headed by Colonel Potter on horseback.

The whole scene brilliantly mixes the iconography and ethos of a Charlie Chaplin comedy (slapstick humor) and a John Ford Western (the last-minute cavalry rescue). Although Margaret greets Burns with a smile, telling him, "We were surrounded by Chinese and they were breathing down our necks," she quickly turns away from him to attend to Potter's call, "Get aboard, Houlihan," and proudly rides with him. In the final analysis, it is Potter (not Hawkeye or Burns), a paternalistic cavalry man who embodies the old chivalric code of honor and duty, who acts as the proper guardian of white female virtue. Margaret's willing submission to Potter's summons of comradeship symbolizes her shift of loyalty from Burns, a villainous clown, to the fraternity of "good guys" who frequently gang up on him.

Her separation from Burns becomes official in the episode that immediately followed, "Margaret's Engagement," in which the head nurse of 4077 gets engaged to Colonel Donald Penobscot in Tokyo. By this point in the series' history, Loretta Swit's Margaret is a far cry from her predecessors in Richard Hornberger's novel and Robert Altman's film. Described as a "femme fatale," Hornberger's "Hotlips" (written as one word rather than two) chastises Hawkeye for letting nurses and enlisted men address him by his first name and is then flatly dismissed by the acidic doctor, who states, "You're a female version of the routine Regular Army Clown. Stay away from me and my gang."[2] Her isolation from the gang is clearly visualized in a corresponding scene of Altman's film. In typical Altman fashion, the soundscape is made up of overlapping voices and sonic transitions, with Hawkeye and Hot Lips's verbal battle in the cafeteria carrying over to the operation room, where the power suddenly shuts off. Everyone carries on with the aid of flashlights and lanterns, singing "When the Lights Go on Again All over the World." Having established a sense of community (to which Hot Lips is denied entry), the camera seamlessly cuts back to the cafeteria. Significantly, in the aforementioned "Bug Out" episode of the TV series, it is Margaret who single-handedly assists Hawkeye and B.J. in surgery while the evacuation staff is busy removing medical equipment and a nearby explosion shakes the OR like an earthquake. To Margaret's question, "Why does the war have to be so noisy?" Hawkeye answers, "That's so you can find it when the lights go out." When the lights did go out in Altman's OR scene, Hot Lips had no place in the sanctified, candlelit community. By contrast, Loretta Swit's sympathetic version of the character stands bravely by the side of Alda's Hawkeye and his incapacitated patient, bringing a light of hope to the darkest moments of uncertainty and fear.

Along with "Bug-Out," another pivotal episode from season 5 signaling the transformation of Margaret Houlihan is "The Nurses." From the opening OR scene, Margaret takes center stage in the narrative. She is apparently restless and frustrated because of the unrelenting summer heat (with the temperature at 110 degrees), not to mention the wretched sanitary conditions of the camp due to a severing of water supplies in the midst of enemy offensives. No one has taken a shower for a week, and the OR "is beginning to smell like the inside of a whale," to borrow Colonel Potter's analogy.

Margaret takes out her anger on the nurses, nitpicking and pointing her finger at them for small mistakes or for their perceived "insolence." Nurse Walsh (Mary Jo Catlett) is slow in refilling blood. Nurse Preston (Patricia Sturges) talks back to Frank (who rudely blames her for his own mistake) and calls him "Mister." Nurse Baker (Linda Kelsey) fails to organize the medical tray. Hawkeye and B.J. gently side with the latter by commenting, respectively, "[That's] just the way I like it," and, "It's the maid's day off." In her pointed response, Margaret asserts her authority over the nurses: "I'll thank both of you to stop interfering with my staff."

Major Houlihan's tension with her nursing staff is exacerbated when she visits their tent that evening to instruct them on their duties for the following day. She opposes their making fudge in the tent, where cooking is forbidden by army regulations, and chastises Lieutenant Gaynor (Carol Locatell) for heavy drinking. The intoxicated nurse defends herself by saying, "I'm numb. I don't even feel sad with burn patients that look like mummies. That's why I'm drinking: to feel something." Then, Margaret redirects her criticism toward Walsh, who has taken peroxide from the supply room to dye her hair blonde. Baker intervenes and insinuates that Houlihan's hair is not natural blonde, either. Margaret takes offense and the two women's argument escalates into a near physical fight. Consequently, Baker is grounded to her tent in the minutes before her husband, Tony (Gregory Harrison), a foot solider, visits the 4077 on his twenty-four-hour leave.

In an effort to materialize a much-needed honeymoon night for the newlyweds (who have been physically separated since their wedding), the ever-resourceful Hawkeye and B.J. devise a scheme to quarantine Tony in Margaret's tent, passing him off as a suspected plague victim in need of around-the-clock observation. Although incredulous, Potter grants their request and orders Margaret to spend the night in the nurses' tent. Lieutenant Baker sneaks out in the middle of the night and joins her husband in Margaret's tent. When she returns to the nurses' quarters at dawn after her blissful (re)union, she is caught by Margaret. The ensuing confrontation scene is the most intense, emotionally charged depiction of female relationships in the entire series.

When Walsh, Preston, and Gaynor gang up, pleading for leniency for their pal Baker, Margaret blames them all for being dishonest with her and tricking her with "another joke, another lie." Baker bounces back, "But how can we be honest with you? You're like a cat waiting for the mice to make a mistake," to which Houlihan answers with the most honest and revealing dialogue ever written for her character: "And do you trust me? You act like I'm the enemy. . . . Did you every show me any kind of friendship? Ask me help with a personal problem? Include me in one of your little bull sessions? Can you imagine what it feels like to walk by this tent and hear you laughing and know I'm not welcome? Did you ever once offer me a lousy cup of coffee?" Delivered with sincerity, dignity, and emotional resonance, this tearful speech serves as a significant turning point in the development of Margaret's character, insofar as she begins to gain the respect and trust of her nurses, whose loyalty previously rested with the "good guys" (Hawkeye, Trapper, and B.J.) rather than with their own oft-vilified or ridiculed boss. Houlihan wins back her female staff once and for all when she protects them by answering Colonel Potter's question about what has happened in her tent: "It's a private matter between me and my nurses."

Margaret's acceptance into this figurative sisterhood is confirmed in the last scene, set in the nurses' tent. Once again the nurses are making fudge, and the major protests, telling them, "Cooking in the tent is against regulations." However, the tension evaporates immediately as Houlihan is invited to join their "bull session" and is offered fudge and coffee. The episode ends with an image of female bonding complete with food, laughs, and small talk. The absence of Hawkeye and the other male characters in these final minutes is conspicuous. "The Nurses" is thus one of the rare attempts by the creators and writers of *M*A*S*H* to shift their focus from the fraternity of doctors to the sorority of nurses. The episode, written by Linda Bloodworth-Thomason and directed by Joan Darling (who had earlier collaborated on CBS's *Rhoda* [1974–78]), also casts sympathetic light on Margaret's alienation among other female members of the 4077 (most disturbingly depicted in the shower scene of Altman's film where Hot Lips's naked body is publicly exposed to the delight of not only diegetic male spectators but also her own nursing staff). Loretta Swit's Houlihan is given a chance to speak out against the cruelty of structured isolation and demonstrate her humane, vulnerable side, winning the sympathy of not only her nurses but also the viewers.

In earlier seasons, Margaret's dominating disposition and strict adherence to army regulations had constantly annoyed and antagonized not only Hawkeye and his cohorts but also the female staff (as one of them states in "The Nurses," "You've ruled, regulated, and reported us to death"). In "Pa-

Major Margaret "Hot Lips" Houlihan bonds with the women on her staff in "The Nurses"

tient 4077," for example, one nurse turns to another after a particularly hard day and says, "Hot Lips Houlihan, blonde landmine"—referring to Margaret's explosive personality, made all the more volatile by her inability to find the expensive ring that Donald has given her (and which has inadvertently been thrown in the garbage by Klinger). In another episode, "Requiem for a Lightweight," Margaret declares to Hawkeye and Trapper, "You stay away from my nurses. They're off limits to you. That's an order." She then transfers their latest object of desire, Nurse Cutler (Marcia Strassman), to another unit against her will. The skirt-chasing doctors express their resentment and disapproval of the meddler; Trapper muses, "That's your basic Hot Lips," to which Hawkeye replies, "I knew a girl like her back in my hometown. Her name was Rover."

As someone who is "frail, vulnerable, [and] sensitive," Margaret spends an awful lot of time fighting for what she thinks is right (a proclivity that Potter links to the Irish American woman's ethnic heritage, in "Souvenirs"). In that respect, then, it is easy to see that she and Hawkeye share certain values. They even share certain drives, as evidenced when Margaret, in "Last Laugh," makes a plea to Potter that she be sent to Tokyo, where her fiancé, Donald, is stationed. Telling her commanding officer that Donald is a virile man who will "go crazy" if she doesn't attend to his (sexual) needs, the head nurse reveals herself to be the one going crazy, rudely telling Radar (who interrupts her plea) to "butt out." "This is man talk," she informs him before trashing Radar's office in a frenzy of anticipated sexual gratification. Only at the end of this episode, once Hot Lips has returned from Tokyo with a blissful smile on her face, is order restored to the 4077, the scene reminiscent of similar ones involving Hawkeye, who likewise achieves peace through sexual intercourse.[3]

While the representation of women in general and "Hot Lips" in particular improved vastly in their textual transmigration from novel and film to television series, Alan Alda's Hawkeye, although a champion of marginalized underdogs (African Americans, Koreans, and lower-ranking enlisted men), does not always express the same degree of respect toward Caucasian women. For instance, when asked by the news correspondent Clete Roberts what he misses most since coming to Korea (in "Our Finest Hour"), Hawkeye responds, "Any woman out of any uniform." Nevertheless, his persona in both the film and television versions of Hornberger's novel is sanitized compared to the original text, wherein the doctor—a married man with two sons back home—engages in several extramarital affairs in Korea and frequently refers to women as "bimbos."[4]

Mobile Army Sexual Hijinks

"I need a nurse of the totally opposite sex!"
Hawkeye, after receiving his monthly
check, in "Pay Day"

"People thought I was Hawkeye."
Alan Alda, interviewed by CNN's Todd
Leopold, "The Truth about Alan Alda"

One of the most significant departures from Hornberger's novel, reflected in both Altman's film and the television series, is the change in Hawkeye's marital status. In the original text, Captain Pierce is married and has two young sons. Also tied down is Duke, a Georgia-born doctor and father of two daughters who was not brought into the television series (owing in part to the character's racial bigotry). In the process of adaptation, the producers and writers of both the film and the TV program opted to transform Hawkeye from an unfaithful husband into a happy bachelor, reflecting to a degree the limitations of neoliberal attitudes in 1970s America. Hornberger's lecherous hero expresses no remorse with regard to his many extramarital affairs in a foreign land and even shares his expertise on the so-called sex game with his equally horny colleagues, stating,

> There are two methods. One is the simple, staid, stateside, hackneyed, civilian approach where you devote all your spare time for a week . . . the second method is quicker and statistically almost as sound. You talk to the broad for a few minutes in some social situation, preferably over a drink, and you say, "Honey, let's go somewhere and tear off a piece." . . . The big plus of this method is that you either score fast or lose fast, and if you lose you can go on to the next blossom without further waste of time, effort, and good booze.[1]

As evidenced in this quote, sex is just another game for Hawkeye—a sport (like golf and football) wherein "scoring" is what matters most.

While Alan Alda's interpretation of the character revels in a fair share of lechery (often disrupted by incoming wounded or other urgent situations), for the most part, Hawkeye's pursuit of the opposite sex is depicted as playful, innocent, and harmless. For example, in a montage sequence from the pilot episode, Hawkeye is shown sneaking up on Lieutenant Dish—popping up from a sleeping bag in her tent and later handing a towel to her in the women's shower stalls. His attempts to snag her attention are rebuffed each time by the lieutenant, who declares that she is "trying to be faithful" to her fiancé and that "a girl can take only so much." However, like Nurse Able (whom Burns dubs "able and willing" because of her apparent readiness to accept sexual invitations in the episode "Hawk's Nightmare"), Dish is burdened by a name that delimits her agency and defines her as an object of male consumption. The clownish bachelor in the TV series is no doubt a more acceptable hero for viewers than the unfaithful married man in the novel. Moreover, the competition between Hawkeye and Trapper (who *is* married) over the same woman is less a dramatic point of contention than a slapstick routine recalling the wholesome gags in classical Hollywood comedies (in the vein of Bing Crosby and Bob Hope's ongoing competition over Dorothy Lamour in their *Road* pictures from the 1940s).

In "Requiem for a Lightweight," Margie Cutler (Marcia Strassman), an attractive new nurse clad only in a shower towel, bumps into Hawkeye and Trapper on her way to the women's quarters. She immediately grabs the attention of both doctors, who start hitting on her. When the embarrassed nurse hastily departs, the shower towel accidentally falls into the grabby hands of Hawkeye, leaving her completely naked offscreen. Gazing in the direction of the unclothed woman, the mesmerized doctors offer a military salute, something they rarely do even to outranking officers. Hawkeye's flirtatious overtures continue in the OR, where he asks Nurse Cutler to address him as "Doctor darling," and orders a kiss in lieu of medical equipment. After the operation, Trapper and Hawkeye begin a mating competition. Holding stolen flowers and stockings, respectively, the two doctors arrive at the same time at the door of Cutler's tent. Hawkeye declares, "It must be obvious even to a moral defective like yourself that we're both zeroed in on the same girl." His tent mate agrees and says that he has a solution: "We'll share her. . . . You take the day watch and I'll take the night."

Nurse Cutler would likely remain safely removed from both pursuers as long as their vigilant stance against one another continues. However, Margaret has already made a preemptive strike and transferred the new nurse to another unit, out of both men's reach. In the wake of this most unwelcome female intervention, male competition quickly transforms into a strategic alliance, with Hawkeye and Trapper now united in the common cause of getting Nurse Cutler back. They strike a bargain with Colonel Blake, who is in desperate need of a pugilist to fight General Barker's prodigy, a gigantic, 260-pound sergeant, in an interunit boxing match. Hawkeye begins training a reluctant Trapper and devises a scheme to sedate the formidable opponent with ether (which they plan to pour on the boxing gloves). When Frank frowns on the plan for being "not very ethical," Trapper plainly replies, "It's not even moral, but we're in a war zone," a comment that reminds us that the heroes of M*A*S*H will not hesitate to cheat or swindle if necessary, since these minor offenses are no more indecent or immoral than the "war game" being played by their own government. Despite the fact that Frank and Margaret sabotage their plans by switching the bottled ether with distilled water, the two doctors ultimately manage to get their nurse back. As soon as Cutler arrives, their temporary alliance ends and competition resumes. To Hawkeye's dismay, Cutler is most impressed with the man who has fought for her, Trapper, and affectionately attends to his bruised face.

The introduction of B. J. Hunnicutt in place of Trapper John McIntyre in season 4 dramatically shifts the moral compass and sexual dynamics of the show. Unlike Trapper, Hunnicutt earns a reputation for being "the most devoted family man in the world," with "an A in fidelity." These words are spoken by Hawkeye in "Hanky Panky," a season 5 episode featuring two subplots involving romantic desire and dedication. The first finds Margaret upset at not having received a letter from her fiancé, Donald Penobscot, in Tokyo. The second involves Nurse Carrie Donovan (Ann Sweeny), who seems preoccupied, lost in thought, in the OR. Conscious of this, B.J. asks her if anything is wrong in the opening scene of this episode, one of the most melodramatic in the entire series and the first to really explore the faithful doctor's internal turmoil following a one-night affair.

After the operation, Hawkeye asks Nurse Donovan out for dinner and a movie, an invitation she turns down, saying

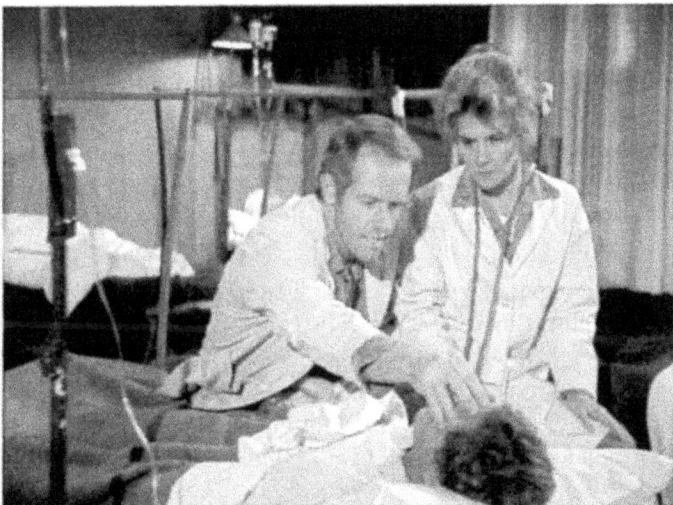

Captain B. J. Hunnicutt and Nurse Donovan in "Hanky Panky"

that she needs to help B.J. in post-op that night. Bewildered, Hawkeye interrogates his friend, asking, "You two got the mutual irresistibles for each other?" He then inquires, "How come she turns down a date with Doctor Jekyll to go work in the lab with Mister Hyde?" This latter remark is significant, since Colonel Blake refers to both Hawkeye and Trapper as "Doctor Jekyll" in the aforementioned "Requiem for a Light-weight." The title of another episode, "Dr. Pierce and Mr. Hyde," makes Hawkeye's penchant for unleashing his id quite clear.[2] In contrast to the two Jekyll-turned-Hydes in *M*A*S*H* (a hedonistic bachelor and a cheating husband), B.J. is considered a wholesome family man who is faithful to his wife in the States. Denying Hawkeye's suggestion that something is going on between Donovan and himself, B.J. asserts, "I'm happily married," to which the cynical bachelor replies, "I thought that was a contradiction in terms."

Later in "Hanky Panky," B.J. ends up falling off "the fidelity wagon" when he visits Donovan's tent to comfort her after she has received a Dear Jane letter from her stateside husband. Following this unplanned one-night stand, he suffers feelings of guilt and tries to write his wife Peg about what has happened. Hawkeye strongly opposes this idea and asks B.J. to take the following vow instead: "I promise to be a good and faithful husband, to write nice, cheerful letters home, to think of Peg often, and to keep my fat hands off Nurse Donovan." Then, Hawkeye himself promises that "someday I will take a vow just like his, Amen," suggesting his conditional willingness to conceive of a future when marital commitment takes precedence over sexual fulfillment. However, the bachelor quickly adds, "But right now, I'm a little late for a very important date."

After evading Nurse Donovan for a week, B.J. finally reconciles with her (in the process learning to forgive himself) and accepts her proposition that they become friends, nothing more.[3] While infidelity is treated lightly as one of many games in the novel and the film—it is lampooned outright in the case of Frank Burns's philandering—the TV episode "Hanky Panky" poignantly captures the emotional repercussions that extramarital affairs bring to wives who are cheated on (represented by Nurse Donovan) and cheating husbands with a guilt-ridden conscience (represented by B. J. Hunnicutt). Hawkeye's vow to take the same oath as B.J. someday is an indication that our hero will eventually become a faithful husband and steadfast father like his fellow Swampman, a radical shift in the course of life set out by the character's creator, Richard Hornberger, who conceived of Hawkeye as an adulterous figure frequently belittling women.

Among this episode's many intertextual allusions is a reference to Mickey Rooney, a star of the Hollywood studio system era who is as famous today for his many failed marriages (seven in total) as he is for the classic films in which he appeared. The reference to Rooney, like those throughout the series to other film and television celebrities as well as historical and literary figures, is meaningful, suggesting that fictional stories—be they filmic or televisual—often tap into very real social problems. The idea that war kills people as well as marriages is made especially compelling by virtue of the dedication of the series' fans to the televisual object of their fascination. Although talking about Altman's filmic adaptation of Hornberger's novel, Robert T. Self's comment that the MASH unit is "an imaginary site where fantasies of rebellion and anxieties about sexual potency can be metaphorically played out" is apropos with regard to the TV show's complex handling of masculinity, which underwent numerous modifications throughout the 1970s but remained as contradictory as the series itself.[4]

Perhaps the most conflicting sites of meaning in M*A*S*H are those moments when Alan Alda's Hawkeye responds to the opposite sex. To better gauge those contradictions associated with a character who—unafraid of showing fear—does not hide behind a shield of "hard" masculinity but instead openly reveals a "soft," feminine side of his personality (one that, ironically, makes his lascivious womanizing less disagreeable), it will be helpful to examine Alda's import as a key player in the cultural rethinking and physical reformulation of the white American male during the 1970s and 1980s.

After his star-making turn as Captain Pierce and his appearances in the comedy-dramas Same Time Next Year (1978) and The Four Seasons (1981), which he also wrote and directed, Alan Alda emerged at the beginning of the 1980s as an unconventional icon for a new generation of men. For many television and film viewers, the gangly, sweater-wearing Alda symbolized a charming alternative to the "Raging Bulls" and "Rockys" of the world: a romantic lead whose masculinity was predicated on sensitivity, intelligence, and roguish wit as opposed to testosterone-fueled machismo and intimidating physical prowess. Even today, despite reputation-shattering forays into more darkly cynical territory (such as his arrogant, self-serving filmmaker in Woody Allen's *Crimes and Misdemeanors* [1989], his greedy, Nobel Prize-minded AIDS researcher in Roger Spottiswoode's *And the Band Played On* [1993], and his war-mongering U.S. president in Michael Moore's *Canadian Bacon* [1994]), Alda's name remains synonymous with humanistic awareness and sensitivity to others, due in no small part to his well-documented personal convictions and political consciousness. This was especially true throughout the run of *M*A*S*H,* a period that saw Alda emerge as an emblematic sign of the late twentieth century's domesticated male—an image that nevertheless presents a rather one-dimensional approach to the actor-director-screenwriter's diverse career and does little to account for the ways his strategic deconstruction of stereotypical masculinity was propelled and shaped by cultural forces.

With the benefit of historical hindsight, it is possible to excavate Alan Alda's entrenched persona and situate it within a broader continuum—a masculine genealogy rooted in everything from the fleet-footed dandyism and finesse of Fred Astaire to the "everyman" earnestness of James Stewart, from the verbal gymnastics and wisecracking of Groucho Marx to the trickster intellectualism of Robert Benchley—while gesturing toward subsequent televisual permutations of the well-read, well-bred "New Man" (culminating in the 1990s with Kelsey Grammer's opera-loving, sherry-sipping character on *Frasier* [NBC, 1993–2004]). This historical continuum furthermore links Alda's East Coast brand of moderate liberalism to that of other outspoken media figures sympathetic to women's rights (such as Ed Asner, Howard Cosell, Phil Donahue, John Lennon, and Gore Vidal). Indeed, the intertextual matrix of meaning surrounding Alda's charismatic persona solidified his status as the ideal, nonthreatening New Man of the 1970s and early 1980s—a hyperconscious manifestation of American masculinity that hearkened back to the male icons of Hollywood's classical studio era (1930s–40s, during which his father, the actor Robert Alda, enjoyed brief success) while suggesting a contemporary concern for civil liberties that could only have emerged in the post-Vietnam, anti-establishment era. The rise of Alda's star status and its eventual decline during the Reagan years thus marked a paradigm shift in the epistemological terrain subtending masculinity studies.

As a longtime advocate of the Equal Rights Amendment (ERA), Alda was able to deploy his New Man image to promote gender equality while refashioning masculinity to accommodate and articulate public dissent. A friend of Gloria Steinem, Alda rose to the top ranks of the profeminist brethren to speak before Senate committees as the chairman of Men for ERA and as a member of Gerald Ford's newly created National Commission for the Observance of International Women. He successfully lobbied against job discrimination, penned several widely circulated essays (among them the Introduction to *A Guide to Non-Sexist Children's Books*), gave inspirational commencement speeches at U.S. colleges,[5] and took great pride in his wife Arlene's successful career as a professional photographer after her twenty years of playing the devoted homemaker (not to mention having given up a chance to play clarinet in the Houston Symphony Orchestra). As reported by a writer for *People* magazine, Alan and Arlene helped "save the deteriorating Seneca Falls, NY home of pioneering 19th-century feminist leader Elizabeth Cady Stanton."[6]

Behind his outspoken attacks on the political status quo was an implicit critique of patriarchal authoritarianism, deflating, as it were, the "masculine mystique" promulgated by his cinematic and televisual forebears. Although a *New York Times* article proclaimed that the aggressively unaggressive Alda—after supplanting John Wayne as America's favorite personality in 1981—had "achieved something close to pop cultural sainthood," not everyone leapt on the bandwagon, particularly those who questioned his sincerity or felt that his celebrity was the result of public relations. Yet Alda persevered and, with the resolve of a self-righteous crusader, stared down the inevitable patriarchal backlash of the 1980s, when rampant "wimp-bashing" and diatribes against "quiche eaters" sparked a nostalgic revival of the conservative ethos and macho posturing of the 1950s.

Besides supporting the women's liberation movement, Alda championed workers' rights, abortion rights, and racial equality (notably, in 1964 he had costarred alongside the African American actress Diana Sands in Broadway's first interracial comedy, *The Owl and the Pussycat*). And yet for all of these admittedly progressive agendas, contradictions linger. As his biographer, Raymond Strait, points out, "It is difficult to understand how anyone with his clout on *M*A*S*H* was so busy selling feminism that he overlooked the lack of it in his own series."[7] Indeed, one of the most obvious contradictions plaguing this series is its writers' willingness to subject female characters to all manner of misogynistic treatment. Are we, like Nurse Sheila Anderson in the episode "Carry on, Hawkeye," supposed to simply take the doctor's flippant remarks and impetuous actions with a grain of salt? Should we just ignore Hawkeye's womanizing and instead focus on his more admirable qualities? Such questions cast light on the underlying contradictions that plague not only the series but also a man who has played everyone from a misogynistic draft dodger in *Jenny* (1970) to a convicted California rapist in *Kill Me if You Can* (NBC, 1977), a made-for-TV movie in which Alda (practically hidden beneath a greasy hairdo and prosthetic nose) utters the line "I am not a sex maniac!" Such a statement might seem ironic in light of Hawkeye's hormonal leanings, but it is deadly serious in the context of a story set in San Quentin (in 1948, two years before the Korean War) that focuses on a wisecracking "rapo" who claims to have an IQ of 140 but refuses the counsel of a female attorney (Talia Shire) even though he is facing the death penalty.

Although Hawkeye, a connoisseur and collector of nudist magazines, never gives up his subscriptions while in Korea, the show did make significant changes in how the character relates to women. These alterations reflect Alda's own gravitation toward and eventual embodiment of a "feminist masculinity" offscreen.[8] Although several episodes between seasons 4 and 6 foretell this transformation, one in particular from season 7 made a significant intervention in Hawkeye's misogynistic tendencies. Broadcast on January 8, 1979, the Emmy-winning "Inga" revolves around Hawkeye's reluctant realization that the newly arrived Swedish surgeon, Inga Helversen (Mariette Hartley), may be a better doctor than anyone else at the 4077, capable of handling tricky procedures like an "end-to-end anastomosis" (an operation that Alda himself would have to undergo years later).

Written and directed by Alda, who dedicated the episode to the memory of Sister Elizabeth Kenney (the British nurse whose experimental procedure for treating polio victims had saved his life years earlier), "Inga" foregrounds a liberated, educated, assertive, and self-possessed woman who is every bit the equal of her male "superiors." Frequently upstaging Hawkeye in the operating room and making sexual advances that derail his own masculine assertiveness, Inga forces the chief surgeon to rethink his preconceived notions of women. That maturation process proves to be quite difficult for Hawkeye, who tellingly proclaims, "I am sex itself, gentleman." These words, delivered to B.J. and Winchester in the opening scene, are the clearest indication of what drives the doctor and will be the basis for measuring Hawkeye's eventual success in both suppressing his libido and performing "plastic surgery on [his] male ego"—a goal he states outright after Margaret and his tent mates give him grief.

By the time the hour-long episode "That's Show Biz" aired three years later (on October 26, 1981), Hawkeye's ego had undergone extensive reconstructive surgery: the character's psychological and emotional trajectory is completely reversed, and it is suggested that he has come to terms with his previous shortcomings. Among the group of touring USO performers who descend upon the camp in this episode is a young singer named Marina Ryan (Gail Edwards), an injured ingénue who falls for Hawkeye during her convalescence. When she first plants a kiss on his cheek, Hawkeye is taken aback. He later tells Marina that his refusal to reciprocate her feelings should not be mistaken as a sign of his lack of interest. Rather, he is doing her a "favor" in not pursuing her, for—as he says to Marina in the penultimate scene—"All you've seen is the bed side of my manner, you haven't seen the bad side. The real Hawkeye Pierce is an egotistical, irresponsible martini guzzler." Informing Marina that he could show her "a roomful of women as lack-of-character witnesses," Hawkeye sums up by stating, "We're the wrong blood type: innocence-positive, lechery-negative." Although Hawkeye often evinces an "ability to cut through his own seriousness with a self-deprecating joke" (something Alda admired in the character),[9] never before had he been so honest about his own shortcomings with the opposite sex.

Of course, that significant moment in the history of M*A*S*H was preceded by several smaller eruptions that show Hawkeye being forced to rethink his attitudes toward women. In "Taking the Fifth," for instance, the unit's nurses gang up on him and take away his expensive bottle of Bordeaux, which he had planned to use as a means of luring just one of them into his arms—a form of bribery that fails because of the women's collective efforts to resist his charms and instill in him a modicum of respect. Hawkeye's earlier obsession with sex, or rather his sexist attitudes (which found their counterpart in the racist comments spewed forth by another unconventional television character of the 1970s, Archie Bunker), was thus incrementally modified over the course of the show's later seasons.

Moreover, we witness during those years brief glimpses of the good doctor in a less-than-flattering light as he falls victim to his childhood neuroses. For instance, he is revealed to be claustrophobic in the season 7 episode "C*A*V*E." The season 9 episode "Bless You, Hawkeye" shows that, after nearly thirty years, he remains psychologically scarred by a prank played on him by his cousin (in which our hero nearly drowned as a young boy). Such moments add texture to an earlier comment uttered by his longtime friend Tommy Gillis in the first-season episode "Sometimes You Hear the Bullet" that Hawkeye "was a bit of a sissy" growing up. As Hawkeye continues to mature in Korea, he begins to embrace his socalled sissiness by tempering the misogynistic aspects of his character and jettisoning pejorative terms like "fairy" (which he utters at one point in the first season).

Corporal Klinger likewise evolves toward the end of the series, but he moves in the opposite direction, largely ditching the outrageous women's attire that had codified him as a "sissy" (or, in Zale's words, a "Hairy Mary") whose only goal was to evade wartime action, in favor of military fatigues in adherence with army regulations. Before Radar's departure and Klinger's promotion to company clerk, the Lebanese American who feigned mental instability in hopes of being sent back to the States seemed to undermine heteronormative conceptions of masculinity associated with classic war films. From the seventh season forward, though, Klinger's "near queerness" is toned down, and in retrospect, his earlier tomfoolery is deemed pathological. As a potentially anarchic and liberating character, he is ultimately brought into alignment with the patriarchal status quo via asymmetrical interactions with men like Potter, who forcefully denies the cross-dressing corporal's request for a Section Eight discharge while retaining an air of benevolence that makes it nearly impossible to dislike him. It is significant that, by the final season, Klinger has stopped wearing women's dresses and has begun exploring a potential love interest in Soon-lee (Rosalind Chao), whom he eventually marries. That cross-cultural wedding—coming after his earlier telephone marriage and messy breakup with his offscreen sweetheart Laverne Esposito—caps his "progress" as a developing character but does so by reinforcing traditional notions of masculinity that are not that far removed from the depictions of men in Hornberger's novel. Indeed, in the aforementioned "Inga" episode, it is Klinger—commiserating with Hawkeye—who states, "Men are men and women are women. You start mixing them up and you won't be able to tell who's who."

One chief difference between the novel and the television show is that the former suggested (in a section dealing with the problems of "Painless" Pole) that homosexual men were not "real men" while the latter proffered a more progressive vision at a time when positive depictions of alternative lifestyles and sexual identities were rare in popular culture. Yet this only compounds the contradictions of a series that often peripheralized and fetishized women yet frequently addressed pressing social issues (such as racism and class warfare) and offered one of American television's first openly gay characters in the season 2 episode "George." By naming that episode after the homosexual Private George Weston (played by Richard Ely), the producers momentarily shifted the narrative focus away from the doctors toward a character who does not reappear in any subsequent episodes but who is a central component in their ongoing efforts to inject occasionally didactic messages about ethical dilemmas and social problems such as bigotry and intolerance. In

Striving for a Section 8: Jamie Farr as Corporal Maxwell Klinger

"George," Hawkeye and Trapper treat two American soldiers who were injured not from gunfire or explosives but rather at the hands of their racist and homophobic peers, who do not take kindly to "colored" people and gay men, and who—like Frank Burns—want to see Weston get a dishonorable discharge from the army.

Significantly, although Klinger is accepted as a member of the *M*A*S*H* "family" (despite his outrageous fashion sense), his "superiors" (the outranking officers) frequently belittle his mental capabilities and make derogatory comments about his physical appearance—comments that revert back to the kind of politically incorrect terminology that the series ostensibly attempts to eradicate. At various times throughout the program's run, Klinger is called such things as a "Lebanese louse" (in "Movie Tonight") and "Tent nose" (in "Letters"). In the season 8 episode "Bottle Fatigue," Charles refers to his stateside sister's Italian fiancé as a "swarthy, dark-haired olive-picker," a remark that then spreads to Klinger once Charles learns that the Lebanese American is actually "half-Italian." Later, in the Swamp, Hawkeye responds to another of Winchester's racist comments, saying, "Spoken like a true patriot, Charles. . . . Red neck, white sheet, and blue nose."

These are the colors of racism, a problem that has plagued American history for centuries. *M*A*S*H* should be applauded for exploring the issues of discrimination and prejudice in such episodes as "The Tooth Shall Set You Free" and "Dear Dad . . . Three," which remind us that the Korean War was the first international conflict in which the United States Army was racially integrated (with African Americans accounting for nearly fifteen percent of all U.S. military personnel stationed on the peninsula). But, as I emphasize in the following chapter, the series should also be scrutinized for its sometimes-problematic depiction of the Korean people and their cultural traditions.

"Another Day in the ROK"

"It's up to us to keep Korea beautiful!"

103

> Klinger to an angry Charles in "The Bill-
> fold Syndrome"

"Welcome to Korea! Land of the Morning
Calm. For 500 years, five centuries, fought
over, mauled and occupied by Mongols,
Manchus, Chinese, Russians, Japanese,
Americans, 16 U.N. countries, and appear-
ing this week only, Professor Jerry
Colonna!"

> Hawkeye's toast to the newly arrived B.J.
> in "Welcome to Korea, Part 1"

"The Americans come here woefully unin-
formed about Korea"

> Kwang-young (Sab Shimono), Charles's
> "houseboy," who, unbeknownst to the
> doctor, is a North Korean spy, in "Dear
> Comrade"

As Elisabeth Weis asserts, at the heart of M*A*S*H's
textual universe are the so-called good guys, the Cau-

casian characters who are defined by "(1) their competence as doctors; (2) their tolerance toward the Other (usually, a Korean peasant or a black solider); [and] (3) their sense of humor."[1] The second classification provided by Weis, related to the doctors' and nurses' benevolence toward so-called "LIPs" ("local indigenous personnel"), invites us to ask how North Koreans and South Koreans figure differently in the novel, film, and television series. What facets of Korean culture, language, and history are on view, and how do they contribute to the episodic narratives in a meaningful, cumulative way? As an extension of these questions, this final chapter also briefly explores the ways in which the presence of additional racial and ethnic "Others" (such as Chinese, Turkish, Greek, or Ethiopian soldiers) further affects how the American characters perceive their own country's interventionist role in a war that was international yet limited in scope.

As paradoxical as *M*A*S*H* is in terms of its simultaneously regressive and progressive constructions of masculinity, femininity, and sexual relations, the series also offers contemporary viewers one of the richest and most complex, if also problematic, arrays of ethnic representations ever committed to film or video. While many critics might take issue with such a claim in light of the series' primary focus on the emotional and physical entanglements of white surgeons and nurses, not to mention Larry Gelbart and Gene Reynolds's professed desire to comment on the situation in Vietnam from an allegorical, antiwar perspective,[2] one cannot ignore the fact that—over the course of its eleven seasons—*M*A*S*H* did more to inscribe the idea of "Korea" in America's collective unconscious than any other cultural production of the twentieth century. It also did more than most to perpetuate stereotypes of Koreans. For instance, the episodes "Mad Dogs and Servicemen" and "Pay Day" suggest that the local people around the 4077 eat canines.

Contradictions are plentiful in *M*A*S*H*, a television series in which the shell-shocked country of Korea is described by sanctimonious American doctors as "medically medieval," "the armpit of the universe," "Hell's outhouse," "a fungus convention in Atlantic City," "the Hoboken of the Orient," "a godforsaken toilet with trees," and "the Detroit of bacteria," yet in which Koreans from both sides of the 38th parallel are frequently treated with respect, dignity, and compassion by the most culturally sensitive surgeons, most notably Hawkeye and B.J., each of whom forges strong, if paternalistic and occasionally patronizing, relationships with local men, women, and children. As Hawkeye sarcastically tells the xenophobic nincompoop Frank Burns in response to the latter's question about why the "yellow Reds" are shooting at them, "I just don't know. . . . All we want to do is bring them democracy and white bread, transplant the American dream: Freedom, achievement, hyperacidity, affluence, flatulence, technology, tension, the inalienable right to an early coronary sitting at your desk while plotting to stab your boss in the back, that's entertainment!"

105

This comment, delivered during surgery in the season 3 episode "O.R.," takes legitimate potshots at the benevolent attitude adopted by the United States government upon realizing that Korea was vitally important to both the cessation of international communism and the midcentury exportation of American culture. Hawkeye's cynical perspective on U.S. interventionism and American values thus confirms and undermines the nation's paternalistic stance toward Korea. Moreover, it lends the neighboring scenes (concerning local "business girls" serving non-Korean soldiers) and references to General Douglas MacArthur's interest in expanding the war into China (as well as his return parade in New York) a metaphorical density that is sometimes lost on media critics who see only the negative aspects of *M*A*S*H,* television's first series to delve into the lives and cultural traditions of Koreans on a continual basis.

One of the most pronounced visual elements in *M*A*S*H* is the presence of the aforementioned "local indigenous personnel" (LIP). This idiomatic expression, used by overseas Americans to refer to Koreans during the war, provides the abbreviated title of a season 2 episode dealing with the marriage of a local woman named Kim and a young draftee, Corporal Phil Walker (Jerry Zaks), who wish to take their newborn baby to the United States. Like the title character in "Kim" (the episode that immediately preceded it in the autumn of 1973), the character named Kim in "L.I.P." is largely a mute bystander whose presence motivates the American surgeons to take some form of action outside the operating room. In the former episode, the silent five-year-old waif becomes the object of Trapper John's paternalistic impulses, leading the doctor to ask his wife by mail if they can adopt the child—a wish that is granted only to be foiled at the end when little Kim's birth mother is located and driven to the camp by a nun. In the latter episode (helmed by the same director, William Wiard), the bride-to-be Kim is referred to by less-sympathetic officers as a "chippie" and a "bimbo"—words that anger Hawkeye and incite him to expedite the bureaucratic paperwork needed to send the interracial couple and their child to America.

By the end of "L.I.P.," Hawkeye has severed his romantic connection to an attractive yet bigoted American nurse, Lieutenant Ginger Bayliss, who is opposed to the couple's marriage. A passage from that penultimate scene reveals just how virulent racist attitudes were among certain Americans during the Korean War:

Ginger: So you had to arrange for a marriage between one of our guys and a gook.

Hawkeye: Kim is Korean.

Ginger: It's a matter of semantics.

Hawkeye: What are you trying to tell me, that you don't care for LIPs?

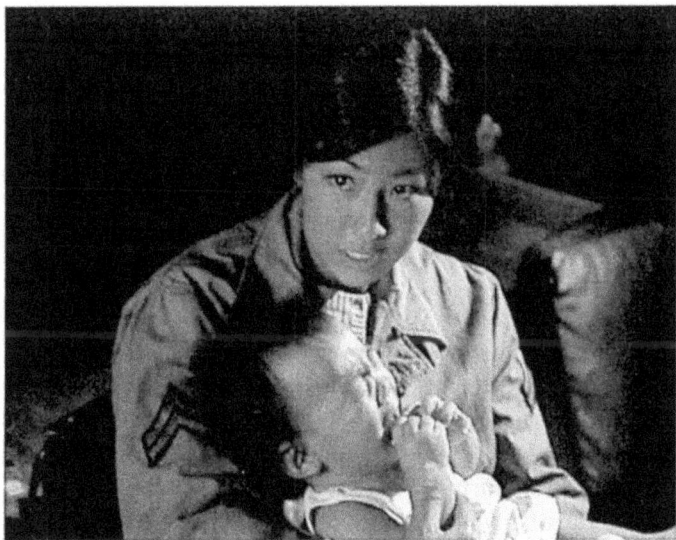

Kim Walker and her newborn baby in "L.I.P."

Newly married couple Kim and Phil Walker in "L.I.P."

Ginger: Not when they marry our people.

Hawkeye: Our people?

This scene, like many others in *M*A*S*H* (especially those involving the cartoonishly hypocritical Frank Burns, who claims to be concerned about the sanctity of marriage as an institution but is having an affair with Hot Lips), juxtaposes Hawkeye's political correctness—his critical questioning of constructed alterity—against an indefensible position, an ideological straw man that can easily be obliterated by, in this episode, the blowing of a raspberry. However, even the most vile and insensitive of characters can force audiences to reflect on the racism, xenophobia, and uncertainties faced by Korean war brides who accompanied their husbands to the United States during the 1950s. For instance, Lieutenant Willis, the man who is brought in to investigate the couple's marriage, finally agrees (under duress) to sign the necessary forms, but in doing so tells Hawkeye, "Let's see [Walker] get an apartment back in the States with a Korean wife!"

Unlike the happy ending of "L.I.P.," which finds Hawkeye and neoliberalist attitudes toward interracial marriage emerging victorious over naysayers like Lieutenants Bayliss and Willis, the conclusion of "Kim" is imbued with sadness, with the sudden feeling of loss experienced by Trapper John as the five-year-old child whom he planned to adopt is taken from him by her birth mother. Having earlier stated that he believes Kim was the reason he was sent to Korea, Trapper is forced to recalibrate his emotions and rationale at the end in order to justify his being there, something that many American military and medical personnel had to do during a war that was for them enigmatic and unclear, a war that was misunderstood by people back in the States and would soon be "forgotten" by nonparticipants.[3]

Adoption and war brides are two of the cross-cultural legacies of the Korean War. The former topic is most assertively foregrounded in "Yessir, That's Our Baby," a season 8 episode directed by Alan Alda that concerns an abandoned Amerasian infant whom the men and women at the 4077 attempt to send to a loving family in the United States only to find that their own government discourages such acts of kindness. However, even in those episodes in which adoption is not really an issue, such as "The Kids," "B.J. Papasan," and "Old Soldiers," the presence of refugee children and impoverished families becomes a means for the white male protagonists to exert their authority and benevolence in spaces where Korean masculinity is either severely undermined or conspicuously absent. In their momentary position as surrogate fathers, B.J., Hawkeye, Colonel Potter, and even the egotistical and snobbish Major Charles Emerson Winchester III come to embody the self-aggrandizing American spirit of the cold war era, even if that means neglecting their other duties and their own physical health.

109

Korean orphans take refuge in the 4077 in "The Kids"

Colonel Potter reading to a group of Korean children in "The Kids"

The theme of romance and the intimation of sexual relationships between American men and Korean women surface in at least two or three episodes each season, most notably "In Love and War," which shows Hawkeye himself succumbing to the charms of an aristocratic yet altruistic woman named Kyung-soon. Played by the then-famous Vietnamese TV personality Kieu Chinh, Kyung-soon may not exactly exude authenticity as a gendered representation of Korea, but her nurturing attempts to serve her impoverished and dying neighbors, young and old alike, not to mention the actress's deftness in communicating emotional truths, which compensates for her inability to speak the Korean language, elevate her performance and suggest a civilized side at odds with the typical imaging of Korean women as "moose" (a GI colloquialism for servants and prostitutes). This humanistic

"In Love and War": Hawkeye's first encounter with Kyung-soon

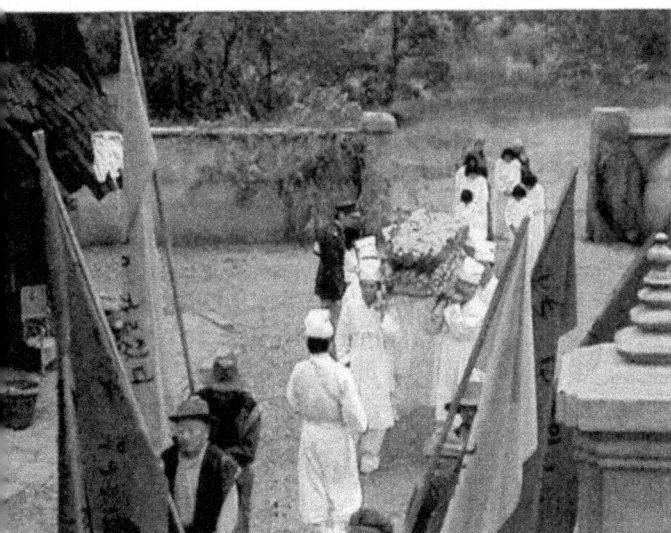

thnographic spectacle: a funeral for Kyung-soon's mother

streak, plus her simple beauty, cast a spell on Hawkeye, the perpetual skirt chaser and loquacious lothario who initially dislikes the Korean woman (whom he mistakenly believes to be petty) but will come to admire and love her by the end of this season 6 episode.

Despite this progressive vision of the white male protagonist's infatuation with and respect for a Korean woman, their prospects of a life together are dim, given the nature of an episodic series in which cast changes or additions were like seismic events for fans who accepted Asian Americans in supporting roles yet apparently were not quite ready for members of this minority group to become romantic leads. Inevitably, "In Love and War" concludes with Hawkeye and Kyung-soon's tearful parting after the death of her elderly mother. Nevertheless, their relationship would linger in Hawkeye's mind and presumably color his subsequent encounters with "local indigenous personnel," beginning with a wounded woman dressed in civilian clothes (Huanini Minn) who—although suspected of being a communist saboteur by a bloodthirsty ROK officer (Mako)—is treated with compassion and care by the doctor in "Guerilla My Dreams."

While Kyung-soon is portrayed as a sophisticated, French-speaking matron of the arts, there are many other, less flattering depictions of Korean women and men that problematize the claim that M*A*S*H puts forth unblemished, positive images without the faintest taint of sexism or racism. In his 1951 book *The Voice of Asia*, James Michener, one of the most prolific and popular postwar American writers and the author of the Korean War novel *The Bridges at Toko-ri* (1953), reports, "Most American military men serving in Korea despised the Koreans . . . [who], being near starvation, stole much American food, and being impoverished stole our equipment."[4] This negative perception of Koreans as thieves, black marketers, or even slave traffickers is put forth in two episodes from season 1 of *M*A*S*H*: "To Market, To Market" and "Moose."

In "To Market, To Market," the 4077 loses two shipments of medical supplies to Korean racketeers. Since their unit desperately needs the two hundred vials of hydrocortisone that were stolen, Hawkeye and Trapper seek to "out-black-market the black market." Armed with Radar's intelligence work, they track down Charlie Lee (Jack Soo), who introduces himself as "the best rep in the Southeast Asia theater of operations." The smooth-talking Swampmen persuade Lee to exchange hydrocortisone (which the black market dealer has already promised to another buyer) for an antique desk that Colonel Blake has recently acquired from the States. Posing as a South Korean general, Lee visits Blake's office to inspect the oak desk before striking a deal. After a series of slapstick sight gags, Hawkeye and Trapper manage to steal the desk and transport it to Seoul by helicopter. Donning an ROK enlisted man's uniform this time, Lee revisits the 4077 to deliver his promised shipment of hydrocortisone in exchange for the antique desk. Spotting the familiar-looking Korean man, Blake—now suspicious—inquires, "Have you got a relative who's a general?" Lee mischievously replies with a knowing smile, "You know how it is, colonel. We all look alike."

This moment is doubly ironic. While the episode self-reflexively pokes fun at the industry's long history of racial/ethnic misrepresentations and the Orientalist notion that "all Asians look alike," its writer (Burt Styler) misidentifies Korea as a *Southeast* Asian rather than *East* Asian region and perpetuates the stereotype of a sinister Orient crowded with criminal syndicates, petty thieves, swindlers, and imposters. Apart from the omnipresent black marketers, impoverished farmers, and pesky peddlers, two major stereotypes of Koreans are highlighted in season 1: "boy-san" and "moose." "Boy-san" was a common appellation for thousands of teenaged Korean houseboys working in American camps during the war. Although Hawkeye and his cohorts call Ho-jon by his first name, someone like him would have been more typically addressed as *boy-san*—a hybrid word rooted in both English ("boy") and Japanese ("san") vocabularies. Similarly, as Radar explains in another episode ("Of Moose and Men"), the mishmash term "moose" derives from the Japanese word *musume* ("daughter" or "young girl"). The term was typically used to refer to a Korean maid or companion who cooked, cleaned, and sometimes even provided sexual services to American soldiers.

While this system of mutual reciprocity has historical grounding in actual U.S. military–Korean civilian encounters during the war and its aftermath, "Moose"—a first-season episode produced before Larry Gelbart and Gene Reynold's research trip to South Korea—grossly caricatures the titular working girl as a submissive, childlike slave who has been sold by her own family for $500 to the bigoted Sergeant Baker (Paul Jenkins). As Hawkeye protests to Baker, the whole concept is both "un-American" and "un-Korean." Although tens of thousands of Korean women and young girls indeed engaged in various types of servile relationships (sometimes monetarily compensated, oftentimes not) with U.S. military personnel before, during, and after the Korean War, it is ludicrous for an American television series otherwise beholden to historical verisimilitude to suggest that any Korean parents would have auctioned off their own daughters to foreign soldiers as portable slaves. The presence of the African American character "Spearchucker" Jones draws an implicit parallel between the "moose" system in Korea and the pre–Civil War slavery system in the Deep South. Jones, who would soon be written out of the series because of Gelbart and Reynold's desire for historical accuracy (since, they argued, no African American doctors were actually stationed in Korea during the war), cynically comments, "I read someplace the U.N. was here to liberate these people. Must have been a misprint."

Conforming to the stereotype of a loyal yet dimwitted slave, Young-hee (Virginia Lee) refuses to be liberated and insists that running away would dishonor her family. Determined to set the Korean girl free, Hawkeye cheats on Baker in a poker game (with the help of Radar peeping at the latter's cards from another tent and radiocasting the information through Hawkeye's hidden earphone). Handed over to Hawkeye in exchange for Baker's two-thousand-dollar debt, Young-hee once again boycotts her own emancipation and declares herself the property of her new master. Having inadvertently become a "moose owner," Hawkeye does a mental run through of some excuses to home (narrated in monologue): "Dear Dad, we had a little poker game today. It seems I won a person. . . . Dear Dad, I know you always wished I had a sister." When Young-hee returns to the camp after being forced to go to Seoul, Hawkeye decides to locate her family through Ho-jon while giving her "demoosifying" lessons.

In a *Pygmalion* mold, he teaches the Korean girl how to speak English in a refined way and how to behave properly in public. This anticipates Major Winchester's brief, nonsexual affair with a Korean prostitute in "Ain't Love Grand," an episode that shows him trying to reform the ill-mannered woman through romantic poetry. As Noralee Frankel argues, "Ain't Love Grand" reveals how, "unlike the usual stereotype, the woman is callously realistic about casual affairs, while the man idealistically refuses to make the distinction between sex and love."[5] At the end of "Moose," Young-hee says, "Shove off"—an American phrase she learned from Hawkeye—to her younger brother Benny (Craig Jue), who, like a pimp, had intended to resell her at a higher price. Instead, she decides to go to convent school where she will study nursing.

115

The episode is problematic in a number of ways. Although it acknowledges the racism of certain American servicemen in the figure of Sergeant Baker (who claims that the "gooks . . . don't mind working"), Koreans are ultimately portrayed as either delinquent child racketeers (boys who sell their own sisters as slaves) or subservient moose who are eager to please white masters and forgo their own liberation. Only after undergoing a deprogramming process that, in this context, can be read as a kind of de-Koreanizing, is Younghee able to reject her kid brother's authority and pursue a life of her own, all thanks to the show's medical heroes and the offscreen American missionary school. In the process of toning down the sexual content of the real "moose" system between American military men and Korean women, the televisual representation turns the legitimate, if exploitative, labor contract into a distorted, anachronistic form of slavery belonging to the cultural imaginary of Southern plantations and frontier pleasure houses from the eighteenth and nineteenth centuries, instead of mid-twentieth-century Korea.

I might also note that the so-called local lovelies on display in the season 3 episode "Iron Guts Kelly," decked out in anachronistic Chinese dresses and referred to at various junctures as "business girls" (by a bourbon-breathed Lieutenant Colonel Henry Blake) and "floozies" (by the dependably uncouth Frank Burns), merely serve as a visual spectacle to be consumed by diegetic as well as extradiegetic audiences. However, as Trapper John states in the same episode, "We are sworn never to misrepresent," a significant line of dialogue that not only reflects the surgeons' jaundiced attitude toward the perpetuation of a myth-making lie (in which the titular Lieutenant General Robert Kelly is said to have died in battle rather than in the heat of passion with Hot Lips) but also insinuates the series' ongoing attempts to curtail what Darrell Hamamoto calls "controlling images" while opening up textual spaces for Asian American actors from various ethnicities to articulate Korean sensibilities.[6] While the only other Asian characters besides the prostitutes in "Iron Guts Kelly"—Mr. Kwok (a bartender in the officer's club, played by Byron Chung) and Mr. Kwang (a fellow doctor, played by Leland Sun)—are peripheral figures with no significant lines of dialogue, several Korean men and women take center stage in subsequent episodes, many of them played by famous Japanese American and Chinese American actors like Clyde Kusatsu, Mako, Pat Morita, Sab Shimono, Jack Soo, and Keye Luke.[7]

Of course, the use of non-Korean actors in the series conforms to Orientalist assumptions about physiognomic similarities and suggests an obliviousness to ethnic difference on the part of mainstream producers and consumers alike. Over the course of M*A*S*H's eleven-year run, such casting decisions resulted in many episodes in which linguistic slippages, sliding ethnocultural signifiers, and untranslated Korean dialogue (sometimes delivered poorly by non-Korean actors) create jarring moments and paint a comic or absurd sonic backdrop—the audio equivalent of those visual ruptures that occur when characters are shown wearing Vietnamese hats and Chinese clothing in crowd scenes. However, as the media scholar Hye Seung Chung has shown in her study of the life and career of the Korean American actor Philip Ahn, this "intermittent transmission of linguistic difference offers distinct reading positions for bilingual, bicultural spectators who harvest meanings out of what initially sounds like incongruous jargon."[8]

As Chung states, "While these floating signifiers (cut free from predetermined and delimiting signifieds) ostensibly construct a monolithic sense of otherness and inscrutability for mainstream audiences, Korean speakers' ears are attuned to the different enunciative patterns of non-Korean actors. In order to fully unpack the multiply signifying images and sounds in M*A*S*H, therefore, it is necessary to address the concept of ethnic reading competency" vis-à-vis episodes that feature Korean characters self-represented by Korean American actors such as Philip Ahn (who, in the twilight of his career, appeared in three episodes of *M*A*S*H*: "Hawkeye," "Exorcism," and "Change Day") and Oh Soon-taek (the most prolific and distinguished Korean actor in Hollywood and television in the years after Ahn's death in 1978).

In an anecdote recounted in Chung's book *Hollywood Asian*, one Korean American commentator, reflecting on his weekly viewings of the series, recollects, "One of the worst experiences for [our family] was watching *M*A*S*H*. These supposedly Korean characters would appear and the non-Korean actors portraying them would mangle Korean language beyond comprehension. This pissed off my parents and me." However, that same viewer (Philip W. Chung) admitted to feeling "proud to be Korean" whenever Oh Soon-taek appeared in the show, "speaking his flawless, dignified Korean—it was exhilarating to see."[9] This particular audience member no doubt took immense pleasure in seeing and hearing Oh Soon-taek perform in "Korean Surgeon," a season 5 episode in which the Japanese-born Korean actor—by then a transnational icon thanks to the commercial success of the James Bond film *The Man with the Golden Gun* (1974)—plays a North Korean doctor named Syn Paek who successfully "passes" as a South Korean thanks to the willingness of Hawkeye and B.J. to maintain the charade. Like many Asian American viewers of *M*A*S*H*, Syn occupies a shifting subject position, one that allows him not only to play the part of a Southerner so as to tend to his wounded countryman but also to see through the charade of his compatriots who are themselves masquerading as South Koreans in hopes of procuring much-needed medical supplies—a ruse that only fans the flames of Frank Burns's suspicion, distrust, and xenophobia.

Dr. Syn Paek was the third of five different characters that Oh Soon-taek played on *M*A*S*H,* immediately preceded by another North Korean—a "savior" of sorts—in an episode from the fourth season titled "The Bus."[10] Although Hawkeye admits in this episode that he has been in South Korea for months and "still can't speak the language," he in fact does know a few words, like *kwenchanayo* ("that's ok") and *kamsahamnida* ("thank you," which, in the episode "Abyssinia Henry," he says to the female proprietor of a local restaurant where three Korean women are brought out to hum the American anthem). B.J., who responds to Hawkeye's earlier comment about not being able to speak the local language by saying, "Well, you Americans figure everybody understands English . . . provided you speak it slowly enough," likewise utters a few expressions in other episodes, such as "The Nurses" and "B.J. Papa-san" (in which the altruistic doctor, who takes a paternalistic interest in a group of waifs, claims that "Hello" and "Put it on Hawkeye's tab" are the only Korean he knows).

119

But of all the men and women at the 4077, Margaret has the greatest command of the language, knowing the words for "Let's go" (*kaja*), "breath" (*sum*), and "I like it" (*choayoh*). These are a few of the Korean expressions she utters in the opening minutes of "The Abduction of Margaret Houlihan," the episode that immediately followed "The Nurses" in 1976 (the year when two American military personnel were killed at P'anmunjom Peace Village, exacerbating tensions between the United States and North Korea) and one that is notable for scenes in which actors of three different ethnicities—Korean (Jane Kim), Japanese (Susan Sakimoto), and Chinese (Le Quyuh)—play Korean characters while the head nurse delivers a baby and Potter provides a birthing lesson to a group of giggling women through the assistance of a South Korean translator (Johnny Yune, a stand-up comedian who gained fame in the 1980s as a frequent guest on Johnny Carson's *Tonight Show*).[11] Potter, as the chief patriarch of the community, is habitually shown training Koreans for various tasks throughout the series, as in "Dear Peggy," an episode that also shows Frank Burns, of all people, teaching locals to speak English.

Until his departure at the end of season 5, Burns—who is compared to General Douglas MacArthur in "Dear Ma"—is the linchpin of the series, someone who represents the "ugly American" at his most chauvinistic. Significantly, like Burns, MacArthur—famous for his trademark pipe and heroic landing at Inch'ŏn—is mocked on numerous occasions throughout the series, as is Senator Joseph McCarthy, whose anticommunist witch hunts in Hollywood as well as in the military were taking place stateside during the Korean War.[12] Occasionally, these infamous figures are mentioned in the same breath, as are Harry Truman and his successor Dwight Eisenhower, U.S. presidents who are not so subtly made the butt of jokes in episodes that tested the permissiveness of political ribbing during the 1970s.[13] Throughout the series, there is a constant stream of satiric wisecracks that underscore the fallibility of political leaders. Again, while such satire was endemic during and just after the Vietnam War era, *M*A*S*H* is filled with direct allusions to people, places, dates, and events that are specific to the Korean War. Seoul, Pusan, Sinch'on, Chuksan, and Ouijongbu (where the 4077 is located until a "bug out" sends the group elsewhere) are just a few of the many cities referred to in the series.[14] In episodes such as "Mail Call, Again" and "The Price," Syngman Rhee—the president of the Republic of Korea—is mentioned, often in a derisive way (as a "dictator").

The P'anmunjom Peace Talks that were held in the demilitarized zone in late October 1951 are referred to in "Dear Mildred," "Peace on Us," and "Hanky Panky," the latter episode forging a connection between the marital breakup of a 4077 nurse and her husband and the dissolution of negotiations that might bring an end to a war that, as one character says, kills both people and marriages. Passing reference is made to the "Little Switch" prisoner exchange in "38 Across," an episode in which the voice of "Seoul City Sue"—an actual radio personality during the war—can also be heard. The episode "Bombed," besides featuring a typically racist comment from Frank Burns (who refers to a wounded North Korean soldier as a "slant-eyed yellow devil"), concludes with a radio broadcast in which Seoul City Sue sarcastically informs American GIs that their wives are having extramarital affairs back in the States. This reference to an actual historical figure, combined with an earlier mention of Bob Hope and his USO show, bookend a story about fear, loss, anger, and ambivalence and ground the narrative with factual details specific to the Korean War.

121

Because the Korean War involved an international coalition of forces, it seems only natural that particular episodes of *M*A*S*H* would gesture toward the contributions of other countries in the United Nations besides the United States, showcasing a Turkish regiment in "A Full Rich Day" and "Post Op," Canadian marines in "Quo Vadis, Captain Chandler," Greek units in "Private Charles Lamb" and "They Call the Wind Korea," an Ethiopian soldier in "O.R.," a wounded Puerto Rican soldier in the aforementioned "Post Op," an oversexed Italian corpsman in "Cementing Relationships," and Sanchez, a Costa Rican nurse in the aforementioned "Bombed." The presence of these and additional ethnic and racial "Others" (including Chinese soldiers aiding the North) illustrates the willingness of Americans to not only acknowledge the United States' interventionist role in a war that was international yet limited in scope but also embrace their own roles in shaping the nation into a properly "pluralistic" society, one that was presumably free of racial intolerance and bigotry.

Of course, such was not the case, as is illustrated in the first episode of *AfterMASH,* CBS's attempt to extend the allure of the original series past its official termination on February 28, 1983, when "Goodbye, Farewell and Amen" was aired. That two-and-a-half-hour final episode of *M*A*S*H*— watched by a record-setting 106 million viewers nationwide and aired thirty years after the armistice was signed (on July 27, 1953)—brought the series to a poignant end. Seven months later, *AfterMASH* debuted to savage reviews on September 26, 1983, around the same time that a Soviet Union interceptor shot down Korean Air Flight 007, not to mention the same year that the nonprofit Korean American Coalition was founded in Los Angeles to support community affairs and civic initiatives. By the time the series was canceled the following year, Korea-related topics had been the focus of many newspaper stories, a few of which reported on the increase in the number of Korean children being brought to the United States by the Holt Adoption Agency and other organizations. In concluding this book, I wish to turn briefly to that much-derided sequel, *AfterMASH,* a short-lived series that reunited Harry Morgan's Sherman Potter and William Christopher's Father Mulcahy with Jamie Farr's ex-cross-dressing Army clerk Klinger and Rosalind Chao's ex-peasant-girl-turned-war-bride Soon-lee, who is shown facing numerous challenges in the United States.

"I Shall (Not) Return"— *AfterMASH*

"Would you believe that two years ago I'd never heard of Korea?"

A wounded soldier speaking to a doctor in "Hawk's Nightmare"

As the second of three CBS spin-offs of *M*A*S*H*, preceded by *Trapper John, M.D.* (1979–86) and followed by *W*A*L*T*E*R* (1984), *AfterMASH* was seen as an obvious attempt by network executives to ride the coattails of the original series.[1] Although riddled with critical bullets after its debut on September 26, 1983, *AfterMASH* lasted an entire season (only one of its thirty episodes never aired). Over the course of that single season, viewers were given a glimpse into the lives of Sherman Potter, Father Mulcahy, and Max Klinger after these three had returned to the United States. Accompanying Corporal Klinger was his Korean bride, Soon-lee, played by the Chinese American actress Rosalind Chao.

Referred to by Robert Lee as "a model of ethnic assimilation," the Korean War bride is often linked to the cold war origins of the model minority.[2] The representation of Soon-

A critical failure (but provocative nonetheless): *AfterMASH*

lee in both *M*A*S*H* and its sequel is indicative of the ways in which that stereotype—the model minority—not only fed into neoliberalist attitudes toward Asian immigrants during the 1950s and 1960s but also continued to animate cultural debates throughout the 1970s and 1980s, when the Korean population in the United States rose to 357,393 (in 1980) before reaching 798,849 (in 1990). Unlike its predecessor, though, *AfterMASH* tackled social problems and identity issues unique to Korean immigrant life in the United States. Indeed, the first episode (written by Larry Gelbart, directed by Gene Reynolds, and titled "September of '53") puts all of its creators' cards on the table and features a scene in which Klinger—after landing in jail for being a bookie and before settling into a lower-middle-class existence with Soon-lee in River Bend, Missouri—appears in court before a judge, where he explains:

I'm a Korean vet. And things haven't exactly been what I thought they'd be while I was over there before I came back home. I remember when the GIs came home after World War II. That was like a hit war, you know. People flew flags. A GI just opened his mouth and somebody put a kiss in it. Now, I didn't expect around-the-clock parading. But I didn't think everyone would go into hiding either. It's like the biggest secret of the Korean War was there was a Korean War. You know what kills me: Nobody calls it that. "Police Action," "Korean Conflict." Take it from me, it was a war. It was dirty. It stunk. At least let's call it what it was. . . . I married a wonderful girl overseas, wonderful. But believe me, Eva Braun wouldn't get the kind of looks she gets over here.[3]

Forcing the viewer to acknowledge not only the widespread cultural misperceptions about the Korean War but also the institutional biases and civil rights violations that Asian immigrants often faced, these lines of dialogue, not to mention subsequent episodes devoted to Soon-lee's efforts to assimilate into the all-white community of River Bend, are important moments in the history of American television, touching on matters of citizenship and pluralism that continue to resonate with contemporary viewers. Nevertheless, most TV reviewers seemed not to care about such things and instead trashed *AfterMASH*. Unlike its renowned predecessor, which dodged cancellation after its first dismal season and managed to score impressive Nielsen ratings from its second season on (not to mention dozens of industry awards and nominations), *AfterMASH* fell from favor and today is remembered as one of the worst spin-offs in TV history. It was not, however, the only attempt to "return" to the original series, whether literally or figuratively.

On February 5, 1980, three years before the end of *M*A*S*H,* CBS stations aired the all-star television special

Because We Care, a benefit concert combined with dramatic and comedic sketches designed to "aid the needy in Southeast Asia." Among the many celebrity performers and presenters taking part in this special at the Dorothy Chandler Pavilion were Julie Andrews, Jane Fonda, Michael Jackson, Walter Matthau, The Muppets, John Ritter, Frank Sinatra, John Travolta, and Danny Kaye, the latter serving as the opening emcee informing the audience about the plight of innocent Cambodian war victims. Clearly echoing some of the epistolary episodes in *M*A*S*H*, Alan Alda appears with Mary Tyler Moore in a short drama about a man and woman separated by wars, communicating through "Dear Jim" and "Dear Ann" letters. In the first section of this sketch, set in 1945, Alda's character—a GI stationed in Burma—receives a stateside letter from his wife referencing the fact that children are begging in the streets of Paris. The second half deals with another letter sent by Moore's character, one that alludes to the senselessness of the "police action" known as the Korean War. His response letter is dated "December 12 or 13, 1968," and in it, he states, "I don't know who the enemy is anymore. I only hope it's not us. . . . It is hard to feel noble about what we're doing." Similar to the way in which Vietnam and Korea are collapsed in this final segment, the two stars join each other on stage and remark to the audience, "The relief of suffering is up to us."

Just as *M*A*S*H* has helped to memorialize the Korean conflict, so too has this most meaningful series about the meaninglessness of war been celebrated as a remarkable achievement in television history. Six months after the final episode "Goodbye, Farewell, and Amen" aired (around the same time that *AfterMASH* was set to debut), the Smithsonian's National Museum of American History paid tribute to the series by showcasing a summer-long exhibition that gave visitors the opportunity to step into the 4077's operating room as well as the Swampmen's tent. Titled "Binding up the

Wounds," this unprecedented celebration of a television show featured near-replicas of the original sets created by the production designer Bert Allen, who traveled to Washington DC to assist in the modification of the Swamp and the OR to fit into the museum's exhibition space. Among the memorabilia accompanying the exhibit, and now contained in the museum's Division of Community Life permanent study collections, were props and paraphernalia (such as Corporal Klinger's dresses and Major Winchester's tape recorder and phonograph) as well as a selection of fan letters, many of which expressed anger and grief about the death of Lieutenant Colonel Blake, whose plane was shot down over the Sea of Japan in the March 18, 1975, episode "Abyssinia, Henry."

One piece of fan mail, written by a female viewer from Pittsburgh, put the commanding officer's tragic death into proper perspective and suggested that it was merely a metaphor for the senselessness of war. Beginning her letter with the words, "For those who claim that death does not belong in comedy, it should be said that comedy does not belong in war," and then—after ruminating on the delicate balance struck by the television series—beseeched its writers and producers not to have Blake be "found alive in the Sea of Japan." Concluding with the statement "It could undo all the good that you did for those of us who have never experienced the terror called war," the audience member—in very simple, very direct words—reminds us that *M*A*S*H* indeed made a difference in how we see the world, how we deal with death, and how we cope with loss in our daily lives.

NOTES

ntroduction

1. *M*A*S*H* was nominated for Outstanding Comedy Series in all but one of its eleven years on CBS, garnering its only Emmy Award in that category in 1974. Rick Moody discusses the popularity of the show in the article "Alan Alda," in *St. James Encyclopedia of Popular Culture,* ed. Sara Pendergast and Tom Pendergast (Detroit: St. James, 2000), 42–43.

2. Peggy Herz, *All about M*A*S*H* (New York: Scholastic, 1975), 3. This book, the first to be published about the series, offers a rare behind-the-scenes glimpse into its production.

3. Noralee Frankel, "The Conscious-Raising of *M*A*S*H*," *Minerva* 1, no. 2 (1983): 68.

   M*A*S*H's legacy has been sustained by syndication, which has made the series a ubiquitous part of the televisual landscape. Beginning in 1979, during its eighth season, the series was released to local stations as an off-network program, one that cost considerably less than other 1970s sitcoms such as *Happy Days* (1974–84) and *Laverne & Shirley* (1976–83). According to Derek Kompare, *M*A*S*H* in syndication "was a juggernaut, 'creaming' the competition no matter when it was scheduled, and earning millions for its syndicators, producers, and star Alan Alda, who had shrewdly acquired back-end profit participation." During the

1980s, only *Three's Company* (1977–84) "rivaled *M*A*S*H* in off-network popularity." See Kompare, *Rerun Nation: How Repeats Invented American Television* (London: Routledge, 2004), 135–36.

4. John Javna and Roland Addad, *Cult TV: A Viewer's Guide to the Shows America Can't Live Without* (New York: St. Martin's, 1985), 178.

5. John Leonard, "Leave It to Cosby," *New York Magazine,* October 22, 1984, 154; Barry Putterman, *On Television and Comedy: Essays on Style, Theme, Performer, and Writer* (Jefferson, NC: McFarland, 1995), 2.

6. Putterman, *On Television and Comedy,* 70.

7. Mike Budd and Clay Steinman, "*M*A*S*H* Mystified: Capitalization, Dematerialization, Idealization," *Cultural Critique* (Fall 1988): 59–74.

8. Budd and Steinman, "*M*A*S*H* Mystified," 71.

9. Quoted in Michael R. Harris, Carl H. Scheele, and Elsa M. Bruton, in "Binding up the Wounds," *National Museum of American History Exhibition Catalogue* (Washington DC: Smithsonian Institution, 1983), 19.

10. Notable publications include: Alan and Arlene Alda's *The Last Days of M*A*S*H* (Verona, NJ: Unicorn Publishing House, 1983), a collection of photos, newspaper clippings, storyboards, and letters that chronicle the final week of shooting the series; David S. Reiss's *M*A*S*H: The Exclusive, Inside Story of TV's Most Popular Show* (New York: Bobbs-Merrill, 1980), a collection of interviews with the producers and cast members; and Suzy Kalter's *The Complete Book of M*A*S*H* (New York: Abradale, 1988), which adds additional interviews (with writers and editors) to the mix alongside detailed plot summaries for the episodes.

11. Jeff Maxwell, *Secrets of the M.A.S.H Mess: The Lost Recipes of Private Igor* (Nashville: Cumberland House, 1997).

12. James H. Wittebols, *Watching M*A*S*H, Watching America: A Social History of the 1972–1983 Television Series* (Jefferson, NC: McFarland, 2003).

13. J. Hoberman, "Only One Catch: Social Influence of the Book *Catch-22*," *ArtForum,* October 1994, 9–10. Hoberman describes Heller's book in a way that suggests the juxtaposition of elements in *M*A*S*H:* "part theater of the absurd, part Phil Silvers sitcom" (10).

14. Rick Mitz, quoted in Wes Gehring, "M*A*S*H Turns 30: The TV Series' Dark Comedy Was a Paean to the Ludicrousness of War," *USA Today,* September 1, 2002.

15. In fact, the Korean War (or "Police Action," as it was called by the Truman administration) has not officially ended. A July 27, 1953, cease-fire brought the actual fighting to a halt, but hostilities remain.

16. Otto F. Apel, *MASH: An Army Surgeon in Korea* (Lexington: University Press of Kentucky, 1998).

17. UCLA's Arts Library Special Collections files contain documents detailing the 1997 trip to South Korea taken by Larry Gelbart, Larry Linville, and David Ogden Stiers, who were invited by the USO and Lieutenant General Richard F. Timmons to commemorate the deactivation of the 43rd Mobile Army Surgical Hospital. This last MASH base on the peninsula, earlier known as the 8055th, fell under the command of the Eighth Army and was the basis for the novel, the film, and the television series. Box 191, folder 6 of the Gelbart files provides information about the visitors' itinerary (shopping in Itaewon, a tour of the Joint Security Area at P'anmunjom, visits to Camp Bonifa and Camp Eagle, and autograph sessions) as well as a ceremony pamphlet listing the day's events on Freedom Field. Also included in the folder is a copy of *Stars and Stripes* (dated June 12, 1997), the front page of which features an article ("Army's Real M*A*S*H Folds with Camp Cast Party") that attests to the lasting importance of the television series to the men and women stationed overseas.

18. See Apel, *MASH: An Army Surgeon in Korea,* 118–19, for more information about the relationships between men and women in the actual 8076th.

19. Apel, *MASH: An Army Surgeon in Korea,* 47–48, 50.

20. Harris, Scheele, and Bruton, "Binding up the Wounds," 24.

21. The offscreen bug outs of another MASH unit, the 8063rd, are occasionally referred to throughout the series (see, for instance, "That's Show Biz, Part 1," "Bombshells," "The Bug Out," and "Dreams"). In the episode "The More I See You," we learn that the 4077 is one of five MASH units stationed in Korea.

22. The 8055th was the first MASH unit deployed in the Korean War, one that had been set up at an American military installation in Yokohama, Japan (Camp Coe), on July 1, 1950, a mere six days after fighting broke out.

23. Reiss, *M*A*S*H*, 122.

24. Kalter, *Complete Book of M*A*S*H*, 29.

Chapter 1

1. Hornberger was one of the 910 reserve doctors stationed in Korea during the war. At the age of twenty-six, the surgical intern was drafted into service and became a member of the 8055 MASH unit, the basis for the fictional 4077. After the success of Robert Altman's 1970 film adaptation of his work, Hornberger—who by then was a thoracic surgeon in Maine—wrote a sequel, *M*A*S*H Goes to Maine,* in 1973.

2. Like Hornberger's *MASH,* Heller's World War II novel *Catch-22* would be adapted into a film in 1970. Directed by Mike Nichols and featuring an ensemble cast of actors, the film starred Alan Arkin as Captain John Yossarian, a protagonist every bit as confounded by his situation as is Hawkeye. While Nichols's adaptation was a box-office disaster, it and Altman's commercially successful *M*A*S*H* share a number of thematic elements, in particular "humor in the face of adversity" (to quote Colonel Cathcart). Also, both feature dense soundtracks in which ambient sounds sometimes drown out the voices of the characters. It is significant that Heller had begun working on *Catch-22* (*Catch-18* in its original draft) back in 1953, the year the Korean War was brought to an inconclusive conclusion with a cease-fire agreement. Although the novel is based on Heller's own experiences as a bombardier in World War II, it is easy to see the text as partially rooted in the quagmire that was Korea given that the absurdities of war were much more evident in this so-called police action than in the international conflicts that preceded it. Indeed, many of the elements incorporated in Heller's novel, such as McCarthy-era loyalty oaths and military advancements in flight (helicopters), are rooted in the cold war ethos of the 1950s, when it was being written, rather than in the World War II era. For an elaboration on the similarities between *Catch-22* and *M*A*S*H*, see J. Hoberman, "Only One Catch: Social Influence of the Book *Catch-22*," *ArtForum,* October 1994, 9–10.

3. Richard Hooker, *MASH* (New York: Perennial, 2001), 110.

4. Hooker, *MASH,* 160.

5. Robert Altman, in *Altman on Altman,* ed. David Thompson (London: Faber and Faber, 2006), 45.

6. Before he made M*A*S*H, Altman had honed his skills as a director, writer, cameraman, and editor of roughly sixty-five industrial films for a company based in Kansas City, then went on to direct episodes for such television series as *Alfred Hitchcock Presents* (CBS, 1955–62), *Bonanza* (NBC, 1959–73), *Combat!* (ABC, 1962–67), and *The Kraft Suspense Theater* (NBC, 1963–65).

7. Notably, Altman opted to minimize Duke's presence in the last thirty minutes of the film. Also worth mentioning is the fact that Tom Skerritt, the actor who played Duke in M*A*S*H, also had a small part in the Korean War film *War Hunt* (1962), in which he played a similar character named Sergeant Stan Showalter.

8. Altman was forced by studio executives to preface his film's first scene with the legend "And then there was . . . Korea" so as to reinforce the idea that M*A*S*H was *not* about the Vietnam War.

9. Douglas Gomery, *The Hollywood Studio System: A History* (Berkeley: University of California Press, 2005), 255.

Chapter 2

133

1. Born Alfonso D'Abruzzo in New York on January 28, 1936, son of the Hollywood character actor Robert Alda, Alan came of age during the Depression, a time that was unkind to millions of Americans and especially to those suffering from debilitating illnesses. Stricken by polio at the age of seven, the young boy lay in bed, paralyzed, for weeks on end. Temporarily crippled at an early age, Alda managed to survive this ordeal after his mother, Joan, decided to try the controversial "Kenney treatment" on him. This procedure, which entailed an almost ritualistic wrapping of the boy's body in scalding hot blankets, was named after a British nurse, Sister Elizabeth Kenney. After months of physical therapy, Alda made a full recovery and was able to use his limbs again. He would carry memories of this experience with him into his adult years. Indeed, when he became one of the most famous doctors on television in the 1970s, Alda would often tell members of the press about Sister Kenney's importance in his life, despite having never met this woman who had been an outsider in the male-dominated medical profession a half-century earlier.

2. Peggy Herz, *All about M*A*S*H* (New York: Scholastic Book Services, 1975), 21.

3. Herz, *All about M*A*S*H,* 23.

4. In "Hawk's Nightmare," Hawkeye describes himself as a "card-car-

rying skeptic," emphasizing his resistance to religious indoctrination.

5. Ironically, this contradicts the characterization of Trapper in Hornberger's novel as the "most urbane of the Swampmen."

6. The unconventional pairing in *The Odd Couple* (which would later inspire Garry Marshall to put a female spin on the story with *Laverne & Shirley* [ABC, 1976–83]) was itself anticipated by earlier shows noted for their multicultural partnerships involving two men from different backgrounds: *I Spy* (NBC, 1965–68) and *Star Trek* (NBC, 1966–69). Several such shows, like *M*A*S*H*, foreground the characters' frustrations in having to share cramped spaces with a member of the same sex. Yet they also elevate the sidekick character above his or her secondary status, placing the figure on nearly equal footing alongside the nominal hero to create a more balanced "buddy system," something anticipated by *I Love Lucy* (CBS, 1951–57). Not surprisingly, in *The Complete Book of M*A*S*H* (New York: Abradale, 1988) Suzy Kalter states, "Trapper played Ethel to Hawkeye's Lucy" (31).

7. Jay Malarcher, *The Classically American Comedy of Larry Gelbart* (Lanham, MD: Scarecrow, 2003), 106.

8. Ironically, one of the most gimmicky elements of *M*A*S*H*—its reliance on epistolary narratives and voiceovers in episodes such as "Dear Dad," "Dear Ma," "Dear Sigmund," "Dear Mildred," "Dear Sis," and "Dear Peggy"—was such an engrained, formulaic facet of the series over the years that it became increasingly difficult for the writers and directors to surprise *M*A*S*H* viewers who had grown accustomed to its many contrivances. However, because these flashback-saturated epistolary narratives filled in important details about different characters' families and backgrounds, they served a specific function in the ensemble series and thus deserve a level of scrutiny that is beyond the scope of this book.

9. Certain words written by Gelbart (such as "dammit," "boobs," and "virgin") would be deleted from the script in accordance with the network's "Program Practices" preproduction guidelines. As Malarcher notes in his biography of Gelbart, the writer responded to the threat of censorship by arguing that such language accurately reflected the situations faced by servicemen and servicewomen during the Korean War and that any compromise would drain "a lot of vitality out of the script" (*Classically American*

10. The lyrics that accompany Mandel's melancholic theme music in the film (later sung during the "last supper" scene) were written by Altman's thirteen-year-old son, Michael. It was thought that the words "suicide is painless" would be inappropriate for a TV theme song, hence their removal.
11. Father Mulcahy's celibacy is put to the test in the season 8 episode "Nurse Doctor."
12. See Otto F. Apel, *MASH: An Army Surgeon in Korea* (Lexington: University Press of Kentucky, 1998), 71–72.

Chapter 3

1. Otto F. Apel, *MASH: An Army Surgeon in Korea* (Lexington: University Press of Kentucky, 1998), 108.
2. Thomas Schatz, "Workplace Programs," in *The Encyclopedia of Television,* vol. 3, ed. Horace Newcomb (Chicago: Fitzroy Dearborn, 1997), 1871.
3. Schatz, "Workplace Programs," 1871.
4. While in many ways a departure from the workplace sitcoms that came in the wake of *The Dick Van Dyke Show,* M*A*S*H helped define the structural parameters of the genre, which, beginning in the late-1970s with the arrival of programs like *Taxi* (ABC, 1978–83) and *WKRP in Cincinnati* (CBS, 1978–82), brought together two seemingly contradictory motifs—conservative family values and a swinging singles lifestyle—at a time when the networks were openly courting a consensus audience. See Barry Putterman, *On Television and Comedy: Essays on Style, Theme, Performer, and Writer* (Jefferson, NC: McFarland, 1995), 101.
5. The season 10 episode "A Holy Mess," in which an AWOL American soldier named Nick Gillis seeks sanctuary in the mess tent-turned-church, clearly illustrates, in spatial terms, just how prone M*A*S*H was to mix secular and spiritual interests.
6. Klinger's constant bid for Section Eight—a reference to Vietnam draft dodgers and army deserters—not only recalls the efforts of twenty-eight-year-old Yossarian to evade military service but also echoes Hawkeye and Trapper's attempt in Hornberger's novel to convince Colonel DeLong that they are "nuts."
7. Klinger was actually created by both Larry Gelbart and Jamie Farr, the former drawing on his memories of a famous Lenny Bruce routine and the latter modifying an earlier character he had

played on *The Red Skelton Show* (CBS, 1953–70). Neither William Christopher nor Jamie Farr was a member of the regular cast during the first three seasons. Only in season 4 (for Farr) and season 5 (for Christopher) were these actors finally accorded that honor.

8. The show never reveals that last name of Kellye, a lieutenant in the army. Although largely relegated to the background, this minor character utters a few lines in several episodes and is even given a close-up in "Mail Call, Again," when she is seen smoking a cigar in celebration of the birth of Potter's granddaughter back in the States. Besides Kellye Nakahara, who played Nurse Kellye in over fifty episodes, several other Asian American actors also appeared as recurring extras in one episode or more of *M*A*S*H*. Joining Nakahara in the nurses' tent was the actress Shari Saba, who appeared in eleven episodes total. Richard Lee Sung could be seen in nine episodes; Eileen Saki in eight episodes. Other actors of Asian descent to appear in more than one episode include Byron Chung, Keye Luke, Philip Ahn, Jerry Fujikawa, Yuki Shimoda, James Saito, and Mako, a Japanese American actor who had earned an Oscar nomination for his role in *The Sand Pebbles* (1966).

9. The origin of McIntyre's nickname, "Trapper," is mentioned in Hornberger's novel, which references an incident in the young doctor's life: a conductor once caught him in a lady's compartment on the Boston & Main train; upon the discovery, his date screamed, "He trapped me!"

10. In the 1970s, Stiers was an actor with limited experience whose only TV roles before *M*A*S*H* had been bit parts in episodes of *Kojak* (CBS, 1973–78), *Rhoda* (CBS, 1974–78), *The Mary Tyler Moore Show* (1970–77), and *Charlie's Angels* (ABC, 1976–81).

Chapter 4

1. Metcalfe also occasionally appeared in episodes from the seventh season onward (he can briefly be seen playing a driver in "The Party," for instance).

2. After a successful second and third season, when it ranked fourth and fifth in the Nielsen ratings, *M*A*S*H* fell to fourteenth place during its fourth season (due in part to CBS's decision to shift the series from Tuesday to Friday nights, where it ran opposite NBC's *Chico and the Man* [1974–78]). The fifth season (when *M*A*S*H* was moved back to Tuesday evenings) marked a resurgence of in-

terest in the show, and each subsequent season saw it return to the top ten most-watched television programs in America (Season 6: eighth place; season 7: seventh place; season 8: fourth place; season 9: fourth place; season 10: ninth place; season 11: third place).

3. Elisabeth Weis, "*M*A*S*H* Notes," in *Play It Again, Sam*, ed. Andrew Horton and Stuart Y. McDougal (Berkeley: University of California Press, 1998), 324.

4. James H. Wittebols, *Watching M*A*S*H*, Watching America: A Social History of the 1972–1983 Television Series* (Jefferson, NC: McFarland, 2003), 138–39.

5. Janet Staiger, *Blockbuster TV: Must-See Sitcoms in the Network Era* (New York: New York University Press, 2000), 3.

6. Limited space prevents me from providing a detailed overview of some of the most pronounced stylistic and thematic elements in *M*A*S*H*, from its reliance on epistolary devices (handwritten letters, voiceover commentaries) and durational extremes (contrasting events and nonevents, intense action and debilitating boredom), to its unremitting focus on drinking, games, familial relationships, and sexual dalliances, to its unprecedented incorporation of thanatological motifs and imagery into the generic universe of the sitcom.

137

Chapter 5

1. Donald McBride, "Broadcast News Coverage of the Korean War," in *Encyclopedia of the Korean War: A Political, Social, and Military History*, ed. Spencer C. Tucker (Santa Barbara: ABC-Clio, 2000), 56.

2. This is detailed in David R. McCann, "Our Forgotten War: The Korean War in Korean and American Popular Culture," in *America's Wars in Asia: A Cultural Approach to History and Memory*, ed. Philip West, Steven I. Levine, and Jackie Hiltz (Armonk, NY: M. E. Sharpe, 1997), 65–83.

3. McCann, "Our Forgotten War," 76.

4. Notable exceptions include those films referencing some of the Korean War's best-known confrontations, such as the Americans' grueling four-month capture and defense of Pork Chop Hill (March 23–July 11, 1953) and the month-long Battle of Heartbreak Ridge (September 13–October 15, 1951). See *Pork Chop Hill* (1959) and *Heartbreak Ridge* (1986), neither of which fea-

tures substantial representations of "local indigenous personnel."
5. McBride, "Broadcast News Coverage of the Korean War," 56.
6. James A. Von Schilling, *The Magic Window: American Television, 1939–1953* (Binghamton, NY: Haworth, 2002), 200–201.
7. Another episode famously telecast *sans* laugh track was the fourth season's "Quo Vadis, Captain Chandler," in which the titular officer (played by Alan Fudge) confounds the camp by claiming to be Jesus Christ. "That's downright blasphemous," Burns utters at one point about this man with a Messiah complex—a sentiment that CBS feared many of the show's viewers would share if the subject were not treated with respect (hence the network's decision to take out the canned laughs).
8. The real-life men and women of the 8063 MASH unit did the same thing (dye everything in the camp red) in their attempt to alleviate the boredom and monotony of their jobs.
9. This line of dialogue anticipates, in "A Holy Mess," B.J.'s reply to the question of how long he and the other staff have been in Korea: "Fifteenth of next month it will be *forever.*"

Chapter 6

1. This motif appears in many episodes in which Hawkeye feels homesick, such as "Sons and Bowlers" and "Hawkeye's Nightmare," the latter featuring a line of dialogue in which the protagonist professes that his biggest hero is his father.
2. Richard Hooker, *MASH* (New York: Perennial, 2001), 60.
3. Although *M*A*S*H* frequently focuses on the doctors' and nurses' carnal desires and adulterous relationships, very rarely does it deal with the topic of sexually transmitted diseases (something only briefly referenced in the episode "Hey Doc").
4. On page 93 of Hornberger's novel, Hawkeye makes the following remark to Trapper, "These bimboes [sic] are on a real Christian kick, so don't disappoint them." On page 142, he states that he and his tent mate are "going to screw the ass off" a young woman.

Chapter 7

1. Richard Hooker, *MASH* (New York: Perennial, 2001), 126–27.
2. The season 6 episode "Dr. Winchester and Mr. Hyde" likewise explores the darker side of Charles, who develops an addiction to amphetamines.
3. Although he remains faithful to his wife after his one night of ro-

mance with Nurse Donovan, B.J. later strikes up a friendship with a female reporter named Aggie O'Shea (Susan Saint James) in the season 8 episode "War Co-Respondent." Directed by Mike Farrell, this episode once again underlines Hunnicutt's ability to stare down temptation.

4. Robert T. Self, "New American Cinema and *M*A*S*H*," in *Robert Altman's Subliminal Reality* (Minneapolis: University of Minnesota Press, 2002), 40.

5. Excerpts from Alda's commencement speech at the Columbia University College of Physicians and Surgeons are included in a short piece titled "A *M*A*S*H* Note for Docs," *Time,* May 28, 1979.

6. Fred Bernstein, "Couples: America's Love Affair with Hawkeye Floats a Movie Hit for Alan and Arlene Alda," *People,* June 15, 1981, 102. In this article, *Ms.* magazine editor Gloria Steinem is quoted as saying, "We might really believe that men were not concerned about the ERA, if not for Alan."

7. Raymond Strait, *Alan Alda: A Biography* (New York: St. Martin's, 1983).

8. For an elaboration of these and other facets of the star's onscreen and offscreen personas, see David Scott Diffrient, "Alan Alda," in *Men and Masculinities: A Social, Cultural, and Historical Encyclopedia,* ed. Michael S. Kimmel and Amy Aronson (Santa Barbara: ABC-Clio 2004), 20.

9. David S. Reiss, *M*A*S*H: The Exclusive, Inside Story of TV's Most Popular Show* (New York: Bobbs-Merrill, 1980), 26.

Chapter 8

1. Elisabeth Weis, "*M*A*S*H* Notes," in *Play It Again, Sam,* ed. Andrew Horton and Stuart Y. McDougal (Berkeley: University of California Press, 1998), 314.

2. The confusion that many audience members experienced with regard to *M*A*S*H's* historical/geopolitical setting is slyly insinuated by Colonel Potter in the episode "Hawkeye Get Your Gun." After spending twenty-four hours in surgery, the frazzled commanding officer asks the titular doctor, "Which war is this?"

3. This sentiment is captured in the season 3 episode "Adam's Rib," when Trapper—telephoning a former "girlfriend" (a three-night-stand named Mildred, which was later to be the name of Potter's wife)—discovers that she and many other people back home do not even know that a war is going on.

4. James Michener, *Voice of Asia* (New York: Random House, 1951), 74.

5. This is not the only time that this mostly celibate man is seen physically as well as mentally engaging the opposite sex (Margaret notwithstanding, who nevertheless has a rather combative and platonic relationship with the Boston blueblood). In "Foreign Affairs," Winchester initially falls for a French Red Cross worker but eventually decides against the relationship after learning about her "Bohemian lifestyle."

6. Darrell Hamamoto, *Monitored Peril: Asian Americans and the Politics of TV Representation* (Minneapolis: University of Minnesota Press, 1995), 2. This book is a groundbreaking examination of Asian Americans in popular media that sheds light on the limited range of representations available to actors of color, which reveal "a plethora of social contradictions that give expression, sometimes unintentionally, to the meaning of [ethnic minorities'] collective presence within the larger society" (2).

7. In "Pay Day," Jack Soo played Kim Chun-kwak, a peddler hawking real as well as fake pearl necklaces. Similarly, the Chinese American screen legend Keye Luke (known to many as Charlie Chan's Son Number One) donned a beard and workingman's *hanbok* as part of his role in the episode "Patient 4077," that of a handyman jeweler named Mr. Shin who not only fashions a specially commissioned surgical clamp for B.J. and Hawkeye but also sells them a replica of Margaret's cheap engagement ring, which Klinger has unwittingly tossed into the trash. Quite often, the actors who were brought on to perform in stand-alone episodes returned to play different characters in later seasons. For example, Clyde Kusatsu plays the decorated war hero Sergeant Yee in the season 8 episode "Goodbye, Cruel World" years after appearing as Kwang-duk in two episodes from the second and third seasons. He then went on to play a Japanese officer, Captain Yamato, in the season 11 episode "The Joker Is Wild." Similarly, Mako starred as Dr. Lin Tam in the season 3 episode "Rainbow Bridge," as Major Choi in the season 5 episode "Hawkeye Get Your Gun," and as the ruthless ROK officer Lieutenant Hung-lee Park in the season 8 episode "Guerilla My Dreams."

8. Hye Seung Chung, *Hollywood Asian: Philip Ahn and the Politics of Cross-Ethnic Performance* (Philadelphia: Temple University Press, 2006).

9. Philip W. Chung, "The Dream Team: Honoring Korean American All Stars," *KOREAM* 12 (January 2000): 14 (quoted in Hye Seung Chung, *Hollywood Asian*, 140).

10. Oh Soon-taek also played Joon-Sung in "Foreign Affairs," Ralph in "The Yalu Brick Road," and Mr. Kwang in "Love and Marriage."

11. Johnny Yune reappeared on the show years later when, in "Comrades in Arms," he played a wounded North Korean whom Hawkeye tends to in a dilapidated hut. The actor's switch from South to North is made all the more ironic by a line delivered by Hawkeye (in response to Margaret's comment that "he's the enemy"): "That's funny, he bleeds just like our side."

12. Nowhere is the mockery of MacArthur more obvious than in the episode "Big Mac," the entire premise of which involves the impending visit of the Supreme Commander to the 4077. "Caesar is coming to inspect us," says one of the draftee doctors—a comment that excites Blake, one of the few times in the series in which the CO acts in a very formal, militaristic way.

    In the episode "Are You Now, Margaret?" the titular nurse, who had once dated someone affiliated with the Communist Party (unbeknownst to her), is investigated as a possible security risk by a congressional aide sent from Washington DC to Korea. When the McCarthy-like stooge tells Hawkeye, "The real enemy we are fighting is within America itself," the doctor responds, "Oh, wait a second. Suddenly, it all makes sense. We're in the wrong country. It's not North and South Korea who should be fighting. Its North and South Dakota."

13. For example, a comment about Dwight D. Eisenhower's impending visit to Korea in "The Late Hawkeye Pierce" inspires the satiric rejoinder, "What's *he* doing coming over here anyway?" Another historical figure mentioned in a number of *M*A*S*H* episodes (such as "Dear Ma," from season 4) is General Matthew Ridgway, the commander of the U.S. 8th Army throughout much of the Korean War who also took over Eisenhower's post as Supreme Allied Commander, Europe, following the latter's presidential election.

14. In "Dear Uncle Abdul," B.J. even improvises a song in the OR— "Mademoiselle from Panmunjom, Oui-jong-bu"—in response to Father Mulcahy's comment that "There's no feeling of unity [in the Korean War], no brave slogans to rally around, like 'Remember Pearl Harbor.'"

Conclusion

1. *Trapper John, M.D.* is sometimes referred to as a "sister series" of *M*A*S*H*, since it features none of the same actors (Wayne Rogers opted not to star in the show, paving the way for Pernell Roberts to take the lead role). *W*A*L*T*E*R*, however, *was* an official spin-off, giving Gary Burghoff the opportunity to reprise his role as Radar O'Reilly, only this time as an unlikely police officer working in St. Louis (rather than his hometown in Iowa) a year after the Korean War ended. Written by *M*A*S*H* alumnus Everett Greenbaum and directed by Bill Bixby, the pilot, which was broadcast on July 17, 1984, was not optioned by network executives. It was the last of *M*A*S*H*'s spin-offs, although there have been several spoofs produced since the mid-1970s, including the short-lived Saturday morning cartoon series *Uncle Croc's Block* (ABC, 1975–76). This latter program features segments titled "M-U-S-H," in which animated canines—or "Mangy Unwanted Shabby Heroes"—named Bulls-eye, Cold-lips, Major Hank Sideburns, Colonel Flake, and Sonar get into trouble and are threatened with disciplinary action by General Upheaval.

2. Robert Lee, *Orientals* (Philadelphia: Temple University Press, 1999), 162.

3. Klinger's sarcastic comments about the Korean War being a "police action" in the first episode of *AfterMASH* recall lines of dialogue from the *M*A*S*H* episode "Dear Uncle Abdul." After B.J. reminds Hawkeye that "this is a police action," Potter interrupts by saying, "You can take it from me, boys and girls, *this is war.* This little set-to is different, though. Seems like the reasons we're here aren't as clear."

Season 1 (1972–1973)
Pilot Episode (September 17, 1972)
"To Market, To Market" (September 24, 1972)
"Requiem for a Lightweight" (October 1, 1972)
"Chief Surgeon Who?" (October 8, 1972)
"The Moose" (October 15, 1972)
"Yankee Doodle Doctor" (October 22, 1972)
"Bananas, Crackers, and Nuts" (November 5, 1972)
"Cowboy" (November 12, 1972)
"Henry, Please Come Home" (November 19, 1972)
"I Hate a Mystery" (November 26, 1972)
"Germ Warfare" (December 10, 1972)
"Dear Dad" (December 17, 1972)
"Edwina" (December 24, 1972)
"Love Story" (January 7, 1973)
"Tuttle" (January 14, 1973)
"The Ringbanger" (January 21, 1973)
"Sometimes You Hear the Bullet" (January 28, 1973)
"Dear Dad . . . Again" (February 4, 1973)
"The Longjohn Flap" (February 18, 1973)
"The Army-Navy Game" (February 25, 1973)
"Sticky Wicket" (March 4, 1973)
"Major Fred C. Dobbs" (March 11, 1973)

"Ceasefire" (March 18, 1973)
"Showtime" (March 25, 1973)

Season 2 (1973–1974)
"Divided We Stand" (September 15, 1973)
"5 O'Clock Charlie" (September 22, 1973)
"Radar's Report" (September 29, 1973)
"For the Good of the Outfit" (October 6, 1973)
"Dr. Pierce and Mr. Hyde" (October 13, 1973)
"Kim" (October 20, 1973)
"L.I.P." (October 27, 1973)
"The Trial of Henry Blake" (November 3, 1973)
"Dear Dad . . . Three" (November 10, 1973)
"The Sniper" (November 17, 1973)
"Carry On, Hawkeye" (November 24, 1973)
"The Incubator" (December 1, 1973)
"Deal Me Out" (December 8, 1973)
"Hot Lips and Empty Arms" (December 15, 1973)
"Officers Only" (December 22, 1973)
"Henry in Love" (January 5, 1974)
"For Want of a Boot" (January 12, 1974)
"Operation Noselift" (January 19, 1974)
"The Chosen People" (January 26, 1974)
"As You Were" (February 2, 1974)
"Crisis" (February 9, 1974)
"George" (February 16, 1974)
"Mail Call" (February 23, 1974)
"A Smattering of Intelligence" (March 2, 1974)

Season 3 (1974–1975)
"The General Flipped at Dawn" (September 10, 1974)
"Rainbow Bridge" (September 17, 1974)
"Officer of the Day" (September 24, 1974)
"Iron Guts Kelly" (October 1, 1974)
"O.R." (October 8, 1974)
"Springtime" (October 15, 1974)
"Check-Up" (October 22, 1974)
"Life with Father" (October 29, 1974)
"Alcoholics Unanimous" (November 12, 1974)
"There Is Nothing Like a Nurse" (November 19, 1974)

"Adam's Ribs" (November 26, 1974)
"A Full Rich Day" (December 3, 1974)
"Mad Dogs and Servicemen" (December 10, 1974)
"Private Charles Lamb" (December 31, 1974)
"Bombed" (January 7, 1975)
"Bulletin Board" (January 14, 1975)
"The Consultant" (January 21, 1975)
"House Arrest" (February 4, 1975)
"Aid Station" (February 11, 1975)
"Love and Marriage" (February 18, 1975)
"Big Mac" (February 25, 1975)
"Payday" (March 4, 1975)
"White Gold" (March 11, 1975)
"Abyssinia, Henry" (March 18, 1975)

Season 4 (1975–1976)
"Welcome to Korea" (September 12, 1975)
"Change of Command" (September 19, 1975)
"It Happened One Night" (September 26, 1975)
"The Late Captain Pierce" (October 3, 1975)
"Hey, Doc" (October 10, 1975)
"The Bus" (October 17, 1975)
"Dear Mildred" (October 24, 1975)
"The Kids" (October 31, 1975)
"Quo Vadis, Captain Chandler?" (November 7, 1975)
"Dear Peggy" (November 11, 1975)
"Of Moose and Men" (November 21, 1975)
"Soldier of the Month" (November 28, 1975)
"The Gun" (December 2, 1975)
"Mail Call Again" (December 9, 1975)
"The Price of Tomato Juice" (December 16, 1975)
"Dear Ma" (December 23, 1975)
"Der Tag" (January 6, 1976)
"Hawkeye" (January 13, 1976)
"Some 38th Parallels" (January 20, 1976)
"The Novocaine Mutiny" (January 27, 1976)
"Smilin' Jack" (February 3, 1976)
"The More I See You" (February 10, 1976)
"Deluge" (February 17, 1976)
"The Interview" (February 24, 1976)

Season 5 (1976–1977)

"Bug Out" (September 21, 1976)

"Margaret's Engagement" (September 28, 1976)

"Out of Sight, Out of Mind" (October 5, 1976)

"Lt. Radar O'Reilly" (October 12, 1976)

"The Nurses" (October 19, 1976)

"The Abduction of Margaret Houlihan" (October 26, 1976)

"Dear Sigmund" (November 9, 1976)

"Mulcahy's War" (November 16, 1976)

"The Korean Surgeon" (November 23, 1976)

"Hawkeye Get Your Gun" (November 30, 1976)

"The Colonel's Horse" (December 7, 1976)

"Exorcism" (December 14, 1976)

"Hawk's Nightmare" (December 21, 1976)

"The Most Unforgettable Characters" (January 4, 1977)

"38 Across" (January 11, 1977)

"Ping Pong" (January 18, 1977)

"End Run" (January 25, 1977)

"Hanky Panky" (February 1, 1977)

"Hepatitis" (February 8, 1977)

"The General's Practitioner" (February 15, 1977)

"Movie Tonight" (February 22, 1977)

"Souvenirs" (March 1, 1977)

"Post Op" (March 8, 1977)

"Margaret's Marriage" (March 15, 1977)

Season 6 (1977–1978)

"Fade Out, Fade In" (September 20, 1977)

"Fallen Idol" (September 27, 1977)

"Last Laugh" (October 4, 1977)

"War of Nerves" (October 11, 1977)

"The Winchester Tapes" (October 18, 1977)

"The Light That Failed" (October 25, 1977)

"In Love and War" (November 1, 1977)

"Change Day" (November 8, 1977)

"Images" (November 15, 1977)

"The M*A*S*H Olympics" (November 22, 1977)

"The Grim Reaper" (November 29, 1977)

"Comrades in Arms" (Part 1) (December 6, 1977)

'Comrades in Arms" (Part 2) (December 13, 1977)
'The Merchant of Korea" (December 20, 1977)
'The Smell of Music" (January 3, 1978)
'Patient 4077" (January 10, 1978)
'Tea and Empathy" (January 17, 1978)
'Your Hit Parade" (January 24, 1978)
'What's Up, Doc?" (January 30, 1978)
'Mail Call Three" (February 6, 1978)
'Temporary Duty" (February 13, 1978)
'Potter's Retirement" (February 20, 1978)
'Dr. Winchester and Mr. Hyde" (February 27, 1978)
'Major Topper" (March 27, 1978)

Season 7 (1978–1979)

'Commander Pierce" (September 18, 1978)
'Peace on Us" (September 25, 1978)
'Lil" (October 2, 1978)
'Our Finest Hour" (October 9, 1978)
'The Billfold Syndrome" (October 16, 1978)
'None Like It Hot" (October 23, 1978)
'They Call the Wind Korea" (October 30, 1978)
'Major Ego" (November 6, 1978)
'Baby, It's Cold Outside" (November 13, 1978)
'Point of View" (November 20, 1978)
'Dear Comrade" (November 27, 1978)
'Out of Gas" (December 4, 1978)
'An Eye for a Tooth" (December 11, 1978)
'Dear Sis" (December 18, 1978)
'B.J. Papa-san" (January 1, 1979)
'Inga" (January 8, 1979)
'The Price" (January 15, 1979)
'The Young and Restless" (January 22, 1979)
'Hot Lips Is Back in Town" (January 29, 1979)
'C*A*V*E" (February 5, 1979)
'Rally Round the Flagg, Boys" (February 14, 1979)
'Preventive Medicine" (February 19, 1979)
'A Night at Rosie's" (February 26, 1979)
'Ain't Love Grand" (March 5, 1979)
'The Party" (March 12, 1979)

Season 8 (1979–1980)
"Too Many Cooks" (September 17, 1979)
"Are You Now, Margaret" (September 24, 1979)
"Guerilla My Dreams" (October 1, 1979)
"Good-Bye Radar" (Part 1) (October 8, 1979)
"Good-Bye Radar" (Part 2) (October 15, 1979)
"Period of Adjustment" (October 22, 1979)
"Nurse Doctor" (October 29, 1979)
"Private Finance" (November 5, 1979)
"Mr. and Mrs. Who?" (November 12, 1979)
"The Yalu Brick Road" (November 19, 1979)
"Life Time" (November 26, 1979)
"Dear Uncle Abdul" (December 3, 1979)
"Captains Outrageous" (December 10, 1979)
"Stars and Stripes" (December 17, 1979)
"Yessir, That's Our Baby" (December 31, 1979)
"Bottle Fatigue" (January 7, 1980)
"Heal Thyself" (January 14, 1980
"Old Soldiers" (January 21, 1980)
"Morale Victory" (January 28, 1980)
"Lend a Hand" (February 4, 1980)
"Goodbye, Cruel World" (February 11, 1980)
"Dreams" (February 18, 1980)
"War Co-Respondent" (March 3, 1980)
"Back Pay" (March 10, 1980)
"April Fools" (March 24, 1980)

Season 9 (1980–1981)
"The Best of Enemies" (November 17, 1980)
"Letters" (November 24, 1980)
"Cementing Relationships" (December 1, 1980)
"Father's Day" (December 8, 1980)
"Death Takes a Holiday" (December 15, 1980)
"A War for All Seasons" (December 29, 1980)
"Your Retention Please" (January 5, 1981)
"Tell It to the Marines" (January 12, 1981)
"Taking the Fifth" (January 19, 1981)
"Operation Friendship" (January 26, 1981)
"No Sweat" (February 2, 1981)
"Depressing News" (February 9, 1981)

"No Laughing Matter" (February 16, 1981)
"Oh, How We Danced" (February 23, 1981)
"Bottoms Up" (March 2, 1981)
"The Red/White Blues" (March 9, 1981)
"Bless You, Hawkeye" (March 16, 1981)
"Blood Brothers" (April 6, 1981)
"The Foresight Saga" (April 13, 1981)
"The Life You Save" (May 4, 1981)

Season 10 (1981–1982)
"That's Show Biz" (October 26, 1981)
"Identity Crisis" (November 2, 1981)
"Rumor at the Top" (November 9, 1981)
"Give 'Em Hell, Hawkeye" (November 16, 1981)
"Wheelers and Dealers" (November 23, 1981)
"Communication Breakdown" (November 30, 1981)
"Snap Judgment" (December 7, 1981)
"Snappier Judgment" (December 14, 1981)
"'Twas the Day after Christmas" (December 28, 1981)
"Follies of the Living, Concerns of the Dead" (January 4, 1982)
"The Birthday Girls" (January 11, 1982)
"Blood and Guts" (January 18, 1982)
"A Holy Mess" (February 1, 1982)
"The Tooth Shall Set You Free" (February 8, 1982)
"Pressure Points" (February 15, 1982)
"Where There's a Will, There's a War" (February 22, 1982)
"Promotion Commotion" (March 1, 1982)
"Heroes" (March 15, 1982)
"Sons and Bowlers" (March 22, 1982)
"Picture This" (April 5, 1982)
"That Darn Kid" (April 12, 1982)

Season 11 (1982–1983)
"Hey, Look Me Over" (October 25, 1982)
"Trick or Treatment" (November 1, 1982)
"Foreign Affairs" (November 8, 1982)
"The Joker Is Wild" (November 15, 1982)
"Who Knew?" (November 22, 1982)
"Bombshells" (November 28, 1982)
"Settling Debts" (December 6, 1982)

"The Moon Is Not Blue" (December 13, 1982)
"Run for the Money" (December 20, 1982)
"U.N., the Night and the Music" (January 3, 1983)
"Strange Bedfellows" (January 10, 1983)
"Say No More" (January 24, 1983)
"Friends and Enemies" (February 7, 1983)
"Give and Take" (February 14, 1983)
"As Time Goes By" (February 21, 1983)
"Goodbye, Farewell, and Amen" (February 28, 1983)

INDEX